How I Became a LIFE MASTER
Playing the WEAK NO TRUMP

How I Became a
LIFE MASTER
Playing the
WEAK
NO TRUMP

Eric v.d. Luft

>> North Syracuse, New York <<
<< Gegensatz Press >>
>> 2006 <<

iv

Cataloging-in-Publication:

Luft, Eric v.d. (Eric von der), 1952-
  How I became a life master playing the weak no trump / Eric v.d.
Luft.
     p. ; cm.
     "A comprehensive exposition of the Kaplan-Sheinwold system,
   incorporating up-to-date aggressive methods."
     Includes bibliographical references and index.
     ISBN 0-9655179-0-X
1. Contract bridge — Bidding. 2. Duplicate contract bridge — Bidding.
3. Kaplan-Sheinwold system (Contract bridge). I. Title.
GV 1282.4 L83h 2005
795.41'52—dc22   AACR2
Library of Congress Control Number 2004099833

First edition, first printing. Printed in the United States of America by
United Book Press, Inc., Baltimore.

The guillemets, or two pairs of opposing chevrons, dark on the lower
cusps and light on the upper, are a trademark of Gegensatz Press.

Distributed to the trade worldwide by:
Gegensatz Press
108 Deborah Lane
North Syracuse, NY 13212-1931

Designed by the author. Printed on acid-free paper. ∞

Contents

This book is for
everyone at
The Bridge Studio,
Syracuse, New York,
and
in memory of
Kenneth V. Santagata

Introduction

This book is for novice and intermediate duplicate bridge players — not for experts. After all, what do I have to tell an expert? I am not one myself, but a solid intermediate[1] who achieved this level of proficiency by consistently taking a modern and rather unorthodox approach to a time-honored system: Kaplan-Sheinwold (K-S). With the possible exceptions of a few nuances in Chapters 5, 6, 11, and 13, experts are already quite familiar with almost everything I have to say. They would likely find more to interest them in the works of Marty Bergen, Ron Andersen, Mike Lawrence, Larry Cohen, or Victor Mollo. But novices and intermediates may find some value in a comprehensive yet simple and direct presentation of a very advantageous system.

The main purpose of this book is to explain this approach to K-S in detail. It presents a complete and coherent theory of aggressive bidding to those non-Life Masters who might be vigorous or creative enough to let it suggest some methods and strategies to help them reach their goal of becoming a Life Master in the American Contract Bridge League.

Besides being intended to encourage would-be Life Masters to improve their bidding, this book is also meant to fill a large gap in the bridge literature: the longstanding lack of a basic sketch of the whole K-S system. Except for Edgar Kaplan's and Alfred Sheinwold's own *How to Play Winning Bridge*[2] and Kaplan's

---

[1] "Solid intermediate" = "a bridge player who is not as good as novices believe and not as bad as experts believe."

[2] First edition: (New York: Fleet, 1958). Revised editions: *How to Play*

little pamphlet, *Kaplan-Sheinwold Updated*,[3] which are clear and interesting, but all out of print, very difficult to find, and rather obsolete, there is no comprehensive or self-contained text where new players can find out much about the weak no trump. Its particulars are conspicuously absent also from Amalya Kearse's *Bridge Conventions Complete*.[4] Of publications in print in 2006, only Judi Radin's nine-page folder, "The Weak No Trump,"[5] and a few sections of *Bridge: Classic and Modern Conventions*,[6] a massive four-volume compendium, offer any modern instruction in this system.

I started playing K-S when I had only about 20 masterpoints, and I have preferred it to all other methods ever since. The main reason I prefer it is because it yields better results. In other words, *it works!*

Bridge and chess are the two great intellectual games. Chess is a war game — probably *the* war game. Bridge, on the other hand, is a communication game. With a limited grammar and a total vocabulary of only fifteen terms — the numbers 1 through 7, the names of the four suits, plus "no trump," "pass," "double," and "redouble" — partners try to establish an implicit deduc-

---

Winning Bridge (New York: Collier, 1962); *The Kaplan-Sheinwold System of Winning Bridge* (New York: Fleet, 1963); *The Kaplan-Sheinwold System of Winning Bridge* (New York: New American Library, 1983, c1963).

[3] (Chicago: Nella, [n.d.]).

[4] Second edition: (Louisville: Devyn, 1990).

[5] (Louisville: Devyn, 1981). No. 19 in the Championship Bridge Series, edited by Ron Andersen.

[6] Edited and published by Magnus Lindkvist (2001-2003).

tive apparatus in order to communicate some very complicated ideas accurately and clearly. Communication,
or the attempt to communicate intelligently with your
partner, is the essence of bridge, not only during the
auction but also by defensive signals during the play.

K-S improves communication between partners
by increasing both the frequency of limit bids and the
frequency of bids in general. You will open many more
hands in K-S than in Standard American bidding. An
initial pass in K-S will therefore usually mean 0-10
high card points (HCP) instead of 0-11 as we expect in
Standard American. This kind of information (the nar-
rowing of ranges) can be important in helping partner
make the right decision.

In addition to being a communication game between you and your partner, bridge can also be a war
game between your side and the opponents. More auctions will be contested with K-S than with Standard
American. As the popularity of aggressive bidding
grows, bridge becomes much more of a war game than
it used to be. Gone are the relatively genteel days of
controlled psychics and solid Roth-Stone openings.

But always remember that there is no substitute
for good play. You will do better in the long run with
bad bidding and good play than with good bidding and
bad play.

Bidding should be determined — not by infatua-
tion with fancy theory or highly complicated systems
— but, purely and simply, as the great Watson wrote
when contract bridge was young, *by the play of the
hand.*[7] *How I Became a Life Master Playing the Weak No
Trump* is a book on bidding. But since the ultimate goal

---

[7] Louis H. Watson, *The Play of the Hand at Bridge*, enlarged and
modernized by Sam Fry, Jr. (New York: Barnes & Noble, 1958), p. 4.
If I were stranded on a desert island with three other bridge players and
thousands of decks of cards and could have only one bridge book, this
is the one I would choose.

of bidding is to get a good result in the play of the hand, as either declarer or defender, please feel free to regard it as an implicit book on the play of the hand too. After all, a sound understanding of bidding in general and especially of the intricacies of your own bidding system, whatever it may be, will help you in the play of the hand, especially when you and your partner find yourselves on defense after a competitive auction.

The purpose of bidding is to give partner accurate information. This is even true when the final decision for the contract, i.e., the captaincy of the auction, is yours, not partner's. If you, as captain, give partner accurate information, then partner's bids, based on your bids, will themselves be more accurate and will thus enable you to make a better decision.

Any bidding system is a language. During the auction, you and your partner are allowed to communicate using only this language, although you may supplement it with English or other appropriate vernacular to provide announcements, alerts, and explanations to the opponents. Like any language, a bidding system consists of a grammar, a semantics, and a deductive apparatus. Its grammar is the fifteen terms along with the rules governing the mechanics of an orderly clockwise auction that ends with three passes. Its semantics is the meaning assigned to each bid, either by treatment, convention, or natural denotation, considered either alone or in a sequence of bids. Its deductive apparatus is its internal logic by which we are each able to draw inferences about the other three hands at the table; for example, if your partner opens 1♠ and you hold 8 HCP and four spades, you can safely infer that the opponents together hold a maximum of 21 HCP and four spades.

You will be presented with a great many conventions[8] and treatments[9] in this book. Some of them may

---

[8] "Convention" = "A partnership agreement about the meaning of a call

seem strange to you. You do *not* need to play all of them in order to play this system! Play only those you are comfortable with. If you feel that you don't need one of them, then don't play it. Play what you know and know what you play. The absolute bare minimum needed to play the weak no trump consists of:

1. The various no trump (NT) opening sequences.
2. Escapes from 1NT doubled.
3. Five-card majors.
4. Plain old Stayman.
5. Plain old Blackwood.
6. Weak two bids.

The system would still be quite basic with the addition of:

1. Negative doubles.
2. Forcing 1NT response to major openings.
3. Inverted minor responses.

All the other conventions and treatments described in this book are just gravy. Don't overtax yourself.

My grandmother taught me (at the age of eight) to play rubber bridge — with four-card majors, short club, 16-18 HCP 1NT opening, intermediate jump overcalls, solid and sound *everything*, and no conventions except Stayman and Blackwood. I had to "unlearn" most of that stuff when I started playing duplicate. Therefore I would like to acknowledge the help given me in my *duplicate* bridge development by Peter Avery, Brad Bagshaw, Jeff Bender, Frank Billera, Carl Burger, Jim Burke, Josh Carino, Dennis H. Cleary, Larry Cohen, Steve Cooper, Frank Dana, Eva Douglas, John and Judy Elliott,

---

unrelated to its natural meaning, e.g., a double jump shift to show a void in that suit and four-card support for opener's suit."

[9] "Treatment" = "A partnership agreement about the interpretation of the natural meaning of a call, e.g., the HCP range of an opening 1NT bid."

Dorothy and Virgil Eveleigh, Joe Fortino, Bill Foster, Art Friday, Bob Garwood, Bernie and Mary Gorkin, Mickey Gutiérrez, John Hackett, Bill Jones, Doug Jones, Eric Kokish, Gerald Lackner, Mike Lawrence, Fran LeBoeuf, Jim Linhart, Mike Lordi, Virginia Luteran, Doug Lyon, John Mace, Jeff Meckstroth, Billy Miller, Geoff Nelson, B. Gayle Phillips, Nancy Pickering, David ("the diabolical") Poriss, Gerry Radway, Bob Rinehart, Bruce Rubin, Ken Santagata, Pierce Smith, Mitch and Donna Snyder, Carole Sutphen, Bob Ternosky, Roz Teukolsky, Alan Truscott, Betty Youmans, and especially Bill Barrington. No one in Syracuse in recent years has done more than Bill to promote bridge among new players.

As my partners and I evolved the way we played K-S into an Aggressive Weak No Trump (AWNT) system, we found that many of our most successful innovations were developed by my frequent and favorite partner, Cameron Ross. Chapter 5 especially, on escapes, owes much to his ideas.

Thanks to Diane and Grace for proofreading the manuscript.

This is a system book. It takes a real expert such as Louis Watson to write a book about the play of the hand, such as Mike Lawrence to write one about strategy and table presence, or such as Eddie Kantar to write one about defense. But anyone who can fill out a convention card and understand the interrelationships among the types of bids listed there can write a system book. Here is mine.

1

The Strategy of Aggression

Ever since the stunning Italian and Chinese victories in the late 1960s and early 1970s, it has been increasingly true that any capable pair of bridge players who conscientiously implement modern scientific bidding theory will — *when left to their own devices* — reach the right contract almost all the time. Moreover, not only the fancy systems like Precision, Matchpoint Precision, and Two-Over-One Game Force, but also modifications and refinements to old workhorses like Kaplan-Sheinwold and even Standard American, are responsible for this remarkable progress in bidding accuracy.

The key to winning bridge when your opponents are (1) capable of doing things right, (2) using a well-developed bidding system, and (3) conscientiously implementing it, is: *Do not leave them to their own devices!*

In other words, open light, preempt often, overcall freely. Get as high as you can as quickly as you can with weak hands and long suits — without sacrificing safety. Use up the opponents' bidding space and break their lines of communication. When they own the deal, start their auction on the 2-level, the 3-level, or even the 4-level as frequently as possible — without sacrificing safety.

A sly declarer can often make 1NT with a combined 18-19 HCP against the defenders' combined 21-22 HCP. Vulnerable, you might be a tad wary of bidding it, but if you bid that contract non-vulnerable with that holding, you are risking 90 vs. -50 or, rarely, -100. The deal really belongs to the opponents, but if you let them bid 1NT you are risking an unlikely 50 vs. a probable -90. It is surely a better matchpoint result to score -50 than -90. So steal the bid! Have no fear that the opponents will double. They usually will not, and even if they do, there are plenty of methods available to escape into a safer suit contract at the 2-level. That is all explained below in Chapter 5.

Basic principles of aggressive bidding include:

Open almost all 11-HCP hands.

When you are non-vulnerable, and especially when they are vulnerable, preempt and overcall on nothing. Do not worry much about suit quality. Any five-card suit will do at the 2-level and any six-card suit at the 3-level.

Bid as often as reasonably possible. Opponents prefer uncontested auctions.

Respect shape and controls more than HCP.

One important warning: If opener opens light, then responder (opener's partner) must be more disciplined, because if both partners are wild, they will too frequently get too high. Similarly, if overcaller overcalls light, then advancer (overcaller's partner) must be the disciplined one, because again there is the danger, if both are wild, of getting doubled too often for big defeats. A wary, reluctant partnership will end up like McClellan at Antietam, unable to take proper advantage of promising situations. A wild, aggressive partnership will end up like Custer at Little Big Horn, slaughtered as soon as the opponents figure out what's what. But the right balance of aggressiveness in opener and over-caller and caution in responder and advancer will carry a partnership to victory like Eisenhower at D-Day, Jackson at New Orleans, or Houston at San Jacinto.

This does not mean that, in a partnership, Fred is always wild and Jim is always cautious. It means that opener and overcaller should usually be wild and responder and advancer should almost always be cautious. It is opener's and overcaller's duty to disrupt the opponents, but it is responder's and advancer's duty to be constructive within the partnership.

So: *opener and overcaller undisciplined; responder and advancer disciplined.* That is one of the most important concepts in this book.

To Open or Not to Open?

One of the main changes I made in my game at just about the time when my bridge playing really started to improve is this: I began to open much more aggressively. Nowadays I open almost every 11-HCP hand. But where do I draw the line?

I would open this 12-count in any seat at any vulnerability, because it has defensive values and because, if partner has as little as ♣AK, or two aces, or three kings, we could even make 1NT. In any case, Opening this hand 1NT will force the opponents to begin at the 2-level and may cause problems for them:

♠ Q J T
♥ Q J T
♦ Q J T
♣ Q J T 9

But I might not be so quick to open this 12-count:

♠ Q J 2
♥ Q J 2
♦ Q J 2
♣ Q J 3 2

I would not open this 11-count vulnerable and I might not open it non-vulnerable except in third seat:

♠ Q J T
♥ Q J T
♦ Q J T
♣ Q T 9 8

And I would never open this 11-count:

♠ Q J 9
♥ Q J 9
♦ Q J 9
♣ Q 9 8 7

The difference, of course, is the spot cards. The tens are usually working; the nines are sometimes; the eights and lower cards are usually not.

The big exception to the principle of not opening ultra-light hands is when you are in third seat after two passes, non-vulnerable, against spineless opponents — in which case you can — and probably should — open almost anything. Once in this situation, with neither side vulnerable, I opened 1♦ with nothing but Axxxxx in diamonds and an outside doubleton queen. When the opponents found out they were missing an ace they stopped short of bidding their cold slam *because they thought I had a full opener!* If I had passed that hand like a good boy, we would have shared a flat result with many other pairs instead of having a top all to ourselves.

Aggressive bidding, especially aggressive opening and aggressive overcalling, will bring you great success in the modern bridge world. Nevertheless, it is wise to define clearly the limits of an aggressive approach. I held this hand sitting West on Board 11 in the July 23, 1993, ACBL International Fund Game:

♠ Q J 6 2
♥ K Q J 6
♦ J 7 5
♣ Q 6

The ACBL analyst wrote: "We fear that some Wests will open on their '12 points'. What ever happened to defensive requirements to begin the auction?" The analyst was afraid that if West opened, then East would become overly encouraged and would push toward a nearly unmakeable 6♠. For once I agree with what I usually consider to be the too conservative analysis of the ACBL commentators on these games. After South dealt and passed, I passed also, and my partner and I ended up at 4♥ (a Moysian fit) making five for a cold top board.[1] My reasoning was that even though I held 12 points, ♦J and ♣Q were practically worthless, and with a pass already on my right, LHO was more likely to have the upper hand on some of my working cards.

We were playing Standard American that night rather than the system I am presenting in this book; but that makes little difference to the argument here. I open aggressively no matter what system I am playing. I just feel safer doing it with K-S. If we had been playing K-S, I would have opened that hand 1NT, a limit bid, thus immediately giving partner enough information to stay out of slam.

Say that you have been dealt an 11-HCP hand. That means that there are 29 HCP left among the other three players at the table. On average, then, each of them will have 9⅔ HCP. You and your partner together will average a combined 20⅔ HCP while the opponents will have only a combined 19⅓ HCP. That is

---

[1] We went on to win the event at our club with a 70.24% game.

somewhere between a jack and a queen, or almost a half-trick worth of difference. If we consider that on average each partnership at the table can expect six-and-a-half tricks at NT,[2] that half-trick difference now means that your side can expect six-and-three-quarters tricks while the opponents can expect only six-and-one-quarter. A good declarer can readily turn that small edge into seven tricks for us and six for them. So what are you waiting for? Get in there and bid!

Each of the thirteen tricks in the 40-HCP deck takes up, on average, 3.0769 HCP. That's about 21½ HCP to take seven tricks at NT. Say you have been dealt a 12-HCP hand. Each of the other three players will average 9⅓ HCP, which means that you and your partner together will have 21⅓. That's only a hair-breadth away from what is needed to make 1NT. So open all — or almost all — 12-HCP hands, even the flat ones, except the worst possible 12-HCP hand, namely, four queens, four jacks, four deuces, and a three.

This kind of aggression at the bridge table is not destructive or nihilistic. On the contrary, it is quite constructive and safe — but just a little bit bolder than most methods. It does not involve or recommend crass overbidding, but rather, studious audacity. It is both mathematically and logically sound, as the above paragraphs show.

The AWNT system provides several major advantages over other systems, mainly in terms of its ability to steal contracts and/or to prevent the opponents from reaching their best contract, while at the same time affording a good degree of safety for its users. But it is not infallible. The following deal illustrates a few possible problems with it:

---

[2] But see Larry Cohen's *To Bid or Not to Bid: The Law of Total Tricks* (Little Falls, N.J.: Natco Press, 1992), pp. 10-11, for a clear explication of how there can be more than thirteen tricks in the deck at suit contracts.

```
Dealer: S          ♠ 9 5 3
Vul.: Neither      ♥ A K 4
                   ♦ T 8 5
                   ♣ A K J 3
```

```
♠ K Q J 7 4              N              ♠ 6 2
♥ T 6                                   ♥ J 8 7 5 3 2
♦ A 4 3          W    ✧    E            ♦ Q J 6
♣ 8 6 4                  S              ♣ T 5
```

```
                   ♠ A T 8
                   ♥ Q 9
                   ♦ K 9 7 2
                   ♣ Q 9 7 2
```

Consider four possible auctions: first, if both pairs use Standard American with opening 1NT range 15-17 HCP:

S	W	N	E
pass	pass	1NT	pass
3NT	pass	pass	pass

Against 3NT played in the North, East would likely lead ♥5. Declarer wins in hand, leads ♦5 at Trick 2 to finesse with ♦K if East covers or with ♦9 if East plays low. North loses this finesse, and at Trick 3, West starts spades. North should duck at least one and probably two spade tricks. After taking ♠A in dummy, North loses one more diamond trick, but takes the rest because East has no remaining entry to West's good spades. Contract made.

Second, if North-South use AWNT and East-West use Standard American:

S	W	N	E
1NT	pass	3NT	pass
pass	pass		

This is a rare case where AWNT hurts North-South while Standard American would have helped them.

West leads ♠K and keeps leading spades until losing to the ace. But West eventually gets in with ♦A to cash long spades for down one.

Third, if North-South use Standard American and East-West use AWNT:

S	W	N	E
pass	1♠ or 2♠³	double	pass
3NT	pass	pass	pass

Finally, if both pairs use AWNT:

S	W	N	E
1NT	2♠	3NT⁴	pass
pass	pass		

3NT played from the North is far from cold, but it is makeable. It is almost impossible played from the South. That is the whole point. An aggressive West, shoving the oar in early, creates a situation in which North-South end up playing their proper contract from the wrong side, thus increasing the chances that East-West will get a plus score.

When I am picking up a new partner at a tournament, I ask the prospect what she would do with this hand in first seat vulnerable:

♠ J x x x x
♥ x
♦ Q x x x x
♣ A K

If she says she would pass, then I will not play with her. If she says she would bid 2♠, then I will. But if she says she would bid 1♠, then I will be thrilled and

---

³ We are not at all reluctant to open a weak two bid with only five pieces. See Chapter 8.
⁴ Lebensohl convention. Fast approach shows values to play 3NT, but without a spade stopper.

delighted to play with her! That's my kind of bidder! Look at that shape and those controls. AWNT uses the Precision method of counting each singleton as 1 distribution point, each doubleton as 3, and each void as 5. So, with all its honors well protected, that's a 14-point hand.

The Rule of 20 is very important for deciding whether to open. It says to open a suited hand at the 1-level if and almost only if the total of its HCP and the total length of its two longest suits equals 20 or more. The following hands qualify:

    ♠ A K Q x x x x x
    ♥ J
    ♦ x x
    ♣ x x

    ♠ Q J x x x x x
    ♥ K J x x x x
    ♦ —
    ♣ —

But these do not:

    ♠ A K Q x x x x x
    ♥ x
    ♦ x x
    ♣ x x

    ♠ —
    ♥ Q J x x x x
    ♦ Q J x x x x x
    ♣ —

The Rule of 20 is not absolute, nor is it the only determinant as to whether to open a borderline hand. It is just a guide. Note that this hand, ♠QJT ♥QJT ♦QJT ♣QJT9, which, as I indicated above on p. 3, I would always open either 1NT playing AWNT or 1♣ playing Standard American, does not meet the Rule of 20. There are other factors to consider, in this case solid sequences and good spots.

The Rule of 20 applies only to suit openings at the 1-level; never to NT openings and especially not to 11½-14 HCP 1NT openings. It applies almost always to shapely hands but less often to flat hands. By the Rule of 20, all 7-HCP hands with two voids should be opened at the 1-level. If your shapely hand does not meet the Rule of 20, consider a preempt. Or rather, don't just consider it. Do it! But not always. The 9-HCP single-suited spade hand on p. 9 is a clear 3♠ or 4♠ opener, depending on partnership agreement,[5] but you should bide your time with the 6-HCP double-suited heart-diamond hand on the same page. Just pass. You may later get a chance to make a very descriptive Michaels or Unusual NT bid, and you will certainly get a chance to come effectively into the auction somehow. *Never open a preempt with a void in your hand!* Your hand is too strong and versatile for that. Just pass and wait.

The old wisdom is that a combined 26 HCP in a partnership's two hands will usually produce game in either NT or a major. That is true, but it will not help you win much nowadays. The new wisdom is that a combined 24 HCP will produce game more often than not, especially when these points are evenly divided, e.g., 12-12, 13-11, or 14-10, rather than 24-0, 23-1, or 22-2. Even when these 24 HCP let you go down, you will not be hurt much, especially at matchpoints and especially in the long run. Whenever my side has a combined 24 HCP, I want to be in game.

We are not quite yet at the stage of wanting to play "All Invitations Forcing," but we have shaded our requirements for bidding game down significantly from standard bidding. If we were playing strong NT openings (15-17 HCP), then, as responder with no four-card major, we would pass with 7 HCP, bid 2NT to invite with 8 (or a good 7), and go directly to 3NT with 9 (or a

---

[5] See the discussion of Namyats in Chapter 8.

good 8). Similarly, playing the weak NT (11½-14 HCP), we pass with 10 HCP, invite with 11 (or a good 10), and jump directly to game with 12 (or a good 11). By "good" in the NT sense, we mean a hand with a runable or easily establishable suit and an entry.

The Principle of Fast Arrival

The Principle of Fast Arrival is one of most helpful, effective, basic, and just plain cool things that you must know about bridge. Obey it and you will not only win boards and matches, but also make friends out of your partners and be in great demand as a partner. Disobey it at your peril! You will not only lose boards and matches, but also make enemies out of your partners and no one will want to play with you.

The Principle of Fast Arrival is quite simple. It says: *If you preempt, never bid again in that auction unless partner forces or invites you to bid.* In other words, if, for example, you open 2♠ and later in the auction freely rebid 3♠ without partner having forced or invited you, then *you should have opened 3♠ in the first place.* You have just given a big gift to the opponents: one level of bidding space that you could just as easily have taken from them by getting to your highest possible level immediately.

The reasoning behind the Principle of Fast Arrival is likewise simple: Good hands are more complex than bad hands. Holding a weak hand with one long suit, there is not much information that you need to convey to your partner. But holding a stronger hand, perhaps with two good suits, good controls, and other helpful aspects, your want to be able to take your time to explore with partner thoroughly and carefully for the best fit at the best level. The former hand can be adequately described in just one bid, but the latter may require several rounds of bidding to describe it well enough to allow you and your partner to establish a reasonable contract.

So bid good or strong hands gradually in order to exchange the maximum of useful information with partner; but zoom into the stratosphere promptly with bad or weak hands in order to deny to your opponents the luxury of that unhindered exchange.

Take the best advantage of specific situations. For example, if partner is a first-seat passed hand and if you are in third seat non-vulnerable while the opponents are vulnerable, then you can do whatever you darn well please.

If all things are equal, you will be dummy 25% of the time, declarer 25% of the time, and defender 50% of the time. In other words, when you are not dummy, you will defend two thirds of the time and declare only one third. Even though it is quite true that bridge matches are won or lost on defense, and that you must be an excellent defender to achieve much in this game, your side is more in control when it declares than when it defends. So try to declare as often as possible, even when you know during the auction that you will most likely go down. *Do not be afraid of going down!* Be afraid of letting the opponents score 110 or 140 against you in a partial when you could have declared for -50 or -100.

This does not mean that you should be a hand hog. Bridge is a partnership game, and partnerships should be give-and-take, not master/servant relationships. The point is to try to get your *side* — not necessarily you yourself — to declare the hand. Either that or cajole the opponents into bidding too high, which can be done in a great variety of ways.

Say you are in third seat with a 2-count. Partner passes. The first word then to flash into your mind should be "Preempt." Why? Because you immediately know — by adding partner's maximum to your count and subtracting that sum from 40 — that the opponents have a *minimum* of 28 HCP (or 27 if partner has a bad 11). You must do something — (almost) anything — to disrupt the opponents along their gold-paved route to at least game and possibly slam. You must do whatever you can to keep them out of their best contract. What? You say you have never made a 4-level jump overcall with Qxxxx, nothing outside, white vs. red? Go for it! — especially if your suit is spades. What can it hurt? Use the Principle of Fast Arrival. Woe to you only if you have 4-3-3-3 distribution. Then you will just have let the opponents go along their merry way.

A good general guide for the practical application of the Principle of Fast Arrival is the well known Rule of One, Two, and Three, which says: With a bad hand at unfavorable vulnerability, preempt expecting to go down one; at equal vulnerability, preempt expecting to go down two; and at favorable vulnerability, preempt expecting to go down three. This rule defines your highest playable level in each of these three situations. A more modern and daring treatment is the analogous Rule of Two, Three, and Four.

But perhaps a better guide than either of these rules may be stated in terms of suit length. This guide works better with preemptive overcalls than with preemptive openings,[6] but still may be applied to openings: With a bad hand, vulnerable, preempt a six-card suit at the 2-level, a seven-card suit at the 3-level, an eight-card suit at the 4-level, etc.; and non-vulnerable, preempt a five-card suit at the 2-level, a six-card suit

---

[6] See Chapter 8 on "Opening Preempts," especially the section on weak twos.

at the 3-level, a seven-card suit at the 4-level, an eight-card suit at the 5-level, etc. Of course, exceptions and adjustments must be considered, e.g., majors are more effective preemptive agents than minors, so you might want to preempt minor suits higher than the guide suggests. Also, you can almost always be crazier in third seat than in any of the other three.

Jamming up the Opponents' Auction

Say that you are in third seat with just 5 HCP and your partner passes in first seat. Or, with the same hand in fourth seat, partner passes after your LHO has passed in first seat. In either case give partner a maximum of 10 HCP.[7] That means that the opponents have a *minimum* of 25 HCP between them. In other words they probably have a biddable, makeable game.

At this point you should always be immediately thinking: "What can I do to disrupt their auction?" Vulnerability does not matter (although you really should be just a tad more careful if you are red and they are white). Your whole thought now should be directed at doing something — anything! — to interfere with their communication. You do not want to just roll over and play dead. It has to be you too. Not partner. Your side cannot afford to wait that long. Partner does not yet have as clear an idea as you do about the division of HCP count between the two sides. Your RHO in second seat will probably take a call. Your RHO in third seat is

---

[7] With a good 11 HCP partner would have opened in our system, and a bad 11 HCP might as well be 10.

practically *bound* to take a call.[8] You must act! If you do not jump into the auction as high as you dare right away, they will very likely find their best game. If you jump in, they may still find it, but not as easily.

So do it! Try to keep them out of game, or at least out of their best game. Try to fool them into thinking that they do not have enough points for game. After all, the opponents do not know — and do not need to know — that you have only 5 HCP. Get crazy! But not too crazy. You do not want to fool partner into thinking you have a good hand.

For example, in third seat, both sides vulnerable, you hold: ♠K9864 ♥52 ♦QT2 ♣T92. Partner passes, RHO opens 1♣. Bid 2♠! What can it hurt? If you get doubled and go down two for 500, they probably could have had 620. If you go down three or four for 800 or 1100, they may have missed bidding a slam. If (as they probably will) they get right back in the auction, you have not lost anything and you have stolen almost two full levels of their bidding space. When I held this hand in the 1996 Oswego Sectional, my LHO bid 3♥ with a 13-count and a decent five-card heart suit. Partner, holding ♠A532 ♥863 ♦J54 ♣Q64, upped my preempt to 4♠. My RHO, with a flat 15-count including ♥AKJ, mulled it over for quite a while before coming out with a bid of 5♥ instead of a double of 4♠. Down one. Top board for us! The par score on this deal is 4♥ making four. Five does not make. We always get a spade, a diamond, and a club. If they had allowed us to play 4♠ doubled, they would have had 1100 for their top board. But that was very difficult for them to know during the auction when we did not leave them enough bidding space to find out.

Sometimes the opponents will make the right decision after your preempt, and you must gracefully ac-

---

[8] If third seat is the third pass, then, with a mere 5 HCP, you can pass out the auction confident of a high board.

cept these losses. This time they did not. They often do not. Aggressive preemptive jump overcalling is a winning strategy in the long run. Risk it!

Here's another case: You are non-vulnerable and they are vulnerable. That's important! You always have a lot more freedom when they are vulnerable and you are not. Use it! In first seat you hold four small spades, five small hearts, three small diamonds, and a stiff small club — a perfect yarborough. After three passes RHO opens 1♣. You know that they have a minimum of 30 HCP between them. Probably only some little flaw prevented RHO from opening 2♣. They may well be headed toward slam. Your job is to stop them from finding it. Bid 2♥! What can it hurt? Partner knows that you are a passed hand, so she will not go crazy and get too high. You will fool the opponents into thinking that you have more points than you do. They will not expect you to jump overcall with a yarborough. You are not worried about the majors. With nine major-suit cards, you have enough to annoy them if they should find a spade fit. They could easily stop in 3NT or 5♣ when 6♣ is cold.

When considering how to disrupt the opponents, do not overlook balancing. The old truism not to let the opponents play below 2NT when they have suit agreement is quite valid. Even at unfavorable vulnerability, do not let them do this. If you are in the pass-out seat when the opponents have bid 1 banana – 2 bananas and your side has passed throughout, you must almost always make a call,[9] regardless of vulnerability. The mere fact that they wanted to pass the auction out at the 2-level marks your partner with some values. Your hand probably has between 6 and 10 HCP. So bid your longest suit if it is at least five cards, even if you have to do it at the 3-level, or reopen with a double if you

---

[9] For an exception, see the section in this chapter on "The Law of Total Tricks," p. 20.

have no five-card or longer suit. The odds strongly favor your side having at least a seven-card fit and 18 or more HCP. The opponents might let you play the contract there, they might bid their own suit up to the 3-level, or they might double you. In the best case scenario, you will push them one level too high; in the worst case scenario, they might score 200, 300, or 500 against you. But those bad results are rare. The point is not to let the opponents play an easy contract, and balancing will achieve that goal most of the time.

Captaincy

When either partner first makes a limit bid, the other partner instantly and almost absolutely becomes the captain of the auction. The limit bidder may not mutiny against the captain's final decision unless the limited hand contains something that the captain could not reasonably have foreseen, for example, a twelve-card fit, a void, an inability to survive at NT, etc.

It does not matter whether the weaker or the stronger of the two hands is the captain. We prefer the stronger hand to declare the contract, but the question of captaincy is irrelevant to the question of who declares. If opener shows a very strong hand, either by opening 2♣, by jumping in a new suit, or by reversing, then responder should make an effort not to be the first to bid NT. NT contracts, especially, almost always play better when the stronger hand remains concealed.

Obeying the principle of captaincy prevents a lot of confusion and partnership misunderstandings. Yet sometimes an auction does not need a captain, i.e., when partners are simply exchanging information with unlimited bids. There is no possible confusion in this

auction: 1♠ - 2♦ - 2♥ - 3♣ - ... Either partner can at
any time shut the auction off at 3NT or refuse to do so.
A natural bid of 3NT ends most auctions. But the 3NT
bidder must accept the fact that as soon as he bids
3NT, he has limited his hand — in this case to around
16 HCP — and has made his partner the captain. If
this partner, the new captain, has extra, previously
unannounced values, she may explore for slam.

Say you have been dealt ♠AKxxx ♥AKxx ♦AKJ
♣J and partner opens a weak two spades. Already the
only question remaining is whether you are going to
bid a small or a grand slam. There is no point in bidding this one slowly and giving the opponents all sorts
of information about controls that they could readily
use on defense. So right away you bid 4NT, implying a
fit and asking for aces. Partner shows no aces. OK,
you are the captain (partner opened with a limit bid).
Generally speaking, continuing Blackwood to ask for
kings guarantees that the side has all four aces. But at
matchpoints if partner has ♣K you want to play this in
6NT rather than in 6♠, accepting the 50% risk that ♣A
will be on your left. Therefore, thanking the bridge
gods that your suit is spades and not clubs, you decide to tell partner a little white lie and ask for kings.
Partner shows no kings. You shut the auction off at
6♠. End of auction. But wait! Out of the blue RHO sac-
rifices at 7♦. Knowing that you are off an ace and that
partner is not void in clubs (or in any other suit, because he opened a weak two, which forbids holding a
void), you double, expecting to reap an excellent matchpoint result. Partner, thinking that our side has all the
aces, and with ♠QJxxxx ♥QJ ♦x ♣Qxxx being fairly
near the top of the HCP range, takes your juicy penalty
double out to 7♠, which is doubled, down one, for a
cold bottom.

The point of this story is that, even though you
lied to partner, you still know partner's hand better

than partner presumes to know yours, you are still the captain, if you had thought your side could make the grand you would have certainly bid it rather than double 7♦. *Partner had no right or reason to mutiny against your final decision!* Partner simply was not privy to as much information about your two hands as you were. That is the nature of limit bidding — and it must be respected.

The Law of Total Tricks

In the mid-1990s Larry Cohen[10] did the whole bridge community a great favor by publicizing and expanding upon Jean-René Vernes's idea that in each deal there is only a fixed number of tricks available to both sides together, and that this number is determined by the combined length of each pair's best trump fit.[11]

For example, if one side's longest fit is eight, and the other side's longest fit is nine, then there are seventeen total tricks available on that deal. If one side can take twelve of them, then the other side can take only five. That means that if the side that can take twelve bids its small slam, then the other side would likely be down seven, i.e., -1700 doubled non-vulnerable, if it sacrificed at the 6-level. Not a good sacrifice! But if one

---

[10] That's Larry Neil Cohen (b. 1959), not to be confused with another bridge champion and author, Lawrence ("Larry") Cohen (b. 1943).

[11] Vernes, a French philosopher, mathematician, and bridge theorist, discovered the Law of Total Tricks about 1955 and introduced it in a series of articles beginning in 1958 and in a book, *Bridge moderne de la défense*, in 1966. It first appeared in English in his article, "The Law of Total Tricks," in the June 1969 *Bridge World*, but it was mostly ignored until Cohen began using it.

side can take ten and the other side can therefore take seven, then if the side that can take ten bids a vulnerable 4♥, the other side, non-vulnerable, should sacrifice at 4♠ if spades are its fit, since down three doubled is only -500. That's a better result than -620. The Law is actually much more complicated than that, but that is the basic idea.

A better guide than the adage not to let the opponents play below 2NT if they have suit agreement is the Law of Total Tricks. A few times it is right to let the opponents play with suit agreement at the 2-level — and not only when they have shown a four-four fit and you are sitting with a stack of five trumps behind declarer. The Law of Total Tricks will tell you when.

Say that LHO in second seat opens 1♣. After partner passes, RHO bids 1♠, which, after you pass, LHO raises to 2♠. After two more passes, you are in the balance seat with ♠AK ♥Qxx ♦xxxx ♣xxxx. Now what?

LHO has exactly four spades. RHO probably does not have more than four, since he did not reraise. You know that partner does not have a stack of spades, since you have two. You also know that he has no five-card suit, because if he did, he would have bid it. He also knows that you have no trump stack and no five-card suit. So, assuming that the opponents' fit is eight, if your longest fit is seven, then there are fifteen total tricks; and if eight, then sixteen. You do not belong at the 3-level unless you want to go down.

Reopen with a double. By now it should be obvious that LHO and partner have the two best hands at the table. Moreover, partner's values are behind LHO's. Partner could either pass for penalty (unlikely), bid 2NT (if he has been trap passing), or (most likely), take you out. The opponents will not double. Your side might go down -50 or -100, but that's better than letting them have their free 110. Yet also by the Law of Total Tricks, you might be making nine when they are making only six or seven.

2

Major Suit Openings

AWNT is strictly a five-card major bidding system. You can play it with any kind of five-card major responses you like, even the most basic set from Standard American. Or you can have them as complicated, artificial, and fine-tuned as you want. But K.I.S.S. ("Keep it simple, Stupid!") is usually good advice.

I almost never open a four-card major. In fact, this admonition is about as close to absolutely "never" as we could ever get in bridge. I cannot remember the last time I opened a four-card major and I can scarcely imagine a situation in which I would do it. The only exception in Standard American might be something like this: ♠Qxx ♥AKQJ ♦xxx ♣xxx. But in our system we would open this hand 1NT!

Responder's first duty is to support opener's major, if possible. But that support does not have to be shown immediately. There are several common situations in uncontested auctions in which responder should make forcing bids in new suits to keep the auction alive until the proper time to show that support. Two examples will suffice:

First, when responder has 10+ HCP, exactly three cards in opener's suit, and no four-card spade suit if opener bid 1♥ or five-card heart suit if opener bid 1♠, the response should be a convenient 2♣ or 2♦, showing at least three cards in the minor. The two-over-one response promises 10+ HCP. Responder's first rebid should then be the cheapest raise of opener's major. If the opening was 1♠ and opener's rebid was 2♥, showing four or maybe five hearts, then responder, holding four hearts and three spades, should show the hearts first, because a four-four fit usually plays better than a five-three fit.

Second, when the opening bid is 1♥, and responder has four or more spades, three or more hearts, and 6+ HCP, she must always bid spades first, even if she has eight hearts and 25 HCP. Showing the spade suit is essential information to convey to partner. Not only is the possible four-four spade important in itself, but even more important is the possibility that the pair might have a double fit in the majors, which would greatly increase the likelihood of being able to pitch or ruff losers in the minors. If opener has five hearts and four spades, and if responder has even the minimum for a double fit, i.e., three hearts and four spades, then the pair together has only ten cards in the minors, which indicates two shapely hands. After responder bids 1♠, opener's first duty becomes to support responder's major, if possible. Thus opener's rebid of anything other than 2♠ in that situation denies having as many as four spades. Upon opener's rebid of 2♠, responder knows about the double fit, so now her first duty becomes to share this new and vital knowledge with opener by bidding hearts at the appropriate level to show her hand strength as well as the heart fit.

Following the principle that responder should be disciplined when opener is undisciplined, this general scheme of responses makes sense:

Pass = 0-5 HCP, no long suit.

Single raise = 6-8 HCP, at least three pieces of trump.

Double raise = limit raise, 9-11 HCP, at least four pieces of trump.

Direct jump to game = 0-9 HCP, at least five pieces of trump, at least one singleton or void.[1]

1♠ (when opening bid is 1♥) = 6+ HCP, at least four spades, forcing.

2♥ (when opening bid is 1♠) = 10+ HCP, at least five hearts, forcing.

2 of a minor = 10+ HCP, at least three cards in the minor, no more than three cards in opener's major, forcing.

Jump shift = 0-9 HCP, at least six cards in the suit, insignificant trump support.

1NT = 5-11 HCP, any distribution, no more than three pieces of trump (standard 1NT forcing).

2NT, 3NT, or double jump shift = response within the Jacoby 2NT system.

In Standard American, a response of 1♠ to an opening 1♥, a response of 2♥ to an opening 1♠, and a response of a minor at the 2-level to an opening of either major are all unlimited and forcing. This standard method is easily adaptable to the AWNT system. But there are many other suit-response methods that are compatible with AWNT, including the whole Two-Over-One Game Force system. Play whichever one you like.

---

[1] This is a very specific standard bid, often misused. Many responders jump directly to game with stronger hands than this, thus shutting opener out and causing the pair to miss some slams. See William S. Root, *Commonsense Bidding* (New York: Crown, 1986), p. 39; or Charles H. Goren, *Goren's New Bridge Complete* (New York: Doubleday, 1985), pp. 33-34.

1 No Trump Forcing and Weak Jump Shifts

The 1NT response to a major suit opening forces opener for one round, shows no more than three pieces of trump, and can show 5-11 HCP with any distribution. But in actual practice it more typically shows 6-9 HCP, because with most 5-HCP hands, lacking good trump support, responder would pass, and with most 10 or 11-HCP hands, responder would make a non-jump bid on the 2-level. That is, the 1NT forcing response to a major shows something between a good, strong, shapely 5-HCP hand and a bad, weak, flat 11-HCP hand, which, again, is tantamount to saying that 1NT forcing responses are done with 6-9 HCP, since we should usually pass with 5 HCP and should usually make a non-jump 2-level response with 10 HCP.

What if you really want to play 1NT after partner opens a major? Say you are an unpassed hand with 8 HCP, one card in partner's suit, three in the other major, four in one minor, and five in the other. Normally a pair would want to declare this deal in 1NT. But we can't. We have given that up. There is no way — unless opener deliberately passes responder's forcing bid — to end the auction in 1NT. So, with that 8-HCP hand, just pass, hoping either that partner has six or more rather than five trumps or that your LHO will balance, which may perhaps, if you are lucky, eventually produce your penalty double of the opponents' contract.

Even if responder is a passed hand, in which case we treat her 1NT response as only semi-forcing, chances are very good that opener will not allow the contract to be played there.

Among the best qualities of 1NT forcing is that it eliminates any reason to use Flannery (a contender, along with Drury,[2] for "World's Worst Convention"). Bad conventions are those which give the opponents too much vital information while giving your partner not enough. They do not survive the cost-benefit analysis.

On the 1-level, whether the opening was a minor or hearts, responder should always prefer to show her four-card major to making any other bid. In order to avoid having to use Flannery, a hand with 5-11 HCP, exactly four spades, and however many hearts, must always respond 1♠, never 1NT or some level of hearts, to an opening 1♥. This way, if a four-four spade fit exists for you, your side will always find it.

Say you have a Flannery hand with 11-15 HCP, exactly five hearts, four spades, and two of each minor. You open 1♥ and partner responds with a forcing 1NT. Now what? You cannot rebid the semi-artificial minor, because you need three cards in the minor for that. You cannot show your spades, because that would be a reverse, and your hand is not strong enough for that. You cannot rebid your hearts, because that would show six. How are you going to lie to partner?

Perhaps you and partner could agree that in this case a rebid of 2♠ by opener would not be a reverse, because opener was forced, had to keep the auction alive, and had no other viable choice. But that would be a bad idea. In the first place, you cannot take a reverse off just by partnership agreement. A reverse is a reverse is a reverse whether you call it that or not. You might as well try to stop the sea. Any non-jump rebid of a second suit by opener which prevents responder from returning to opener's first suit below the 3-level on the second round of bidding is a reverse — and requires opener to have at least an ace above an opening count. If you don't have it, don't bid it.

---

[2] Drury tells partner whether your opening was light or sound; but, since we expect all our openings to be light anyway, and respond accordingly, why should we tell the opponents something about our hands that we ourselves do not need to know?

But why should opener care about the spade suit anyway? Responder, by bidding 1NT forcing, has already denied having as many as four spades, so the pair has at best a four-three spade fit. Therefore opener should just rebid 2NT, which describes the hand and does not rule out for responder the possibility that opener holds four spades.

Responder's rebid of 3 of opener's major after a response of 1NT forcing shows 9-11 HCP with trump support. If opener's rebid was either a second suit or 2NT, either of which would show exactly five pieces of trump, then responder's rebid is the equivalent of a limit raise with only three pieces of trump. If opener's rebid was the original suit, showing six or more pieces of trump, then responder's rebid promises only two pieces, though the hand may still contain three.[3]

Say partner opens 1♥ or 1♠ and you respond 1NT forcing. If his rebid shows minimum values, then your rebid of 3 of his major is invitational, promising maximum values and two trumps (if he has shown six or more) or three trumps (in all other cases). Partner should accept the invitation with either 14 HCP or a good 13. Remember, we want to be in game whenever our side has a combined 24 HCP.

Responder's rebid of 2 of opener's major — if this bid is still available — shows 5-8 HCP with exactly two pieces of trump. If responder had three trumps, she would have either passed with 5 HCP or given opener a single raise with 6-8 HCP, rather than bid 1NT at all.

If 1NT forcing is played in conjunction with weak jump shifts, then the longest of the three other suits in responder's hand would usually not be longer than five cards, especially at the lower end of the HCP range for the 1NT response. If responder had a weak hand with

---

[3] See William S. Root and Richard Pavlicek, *Modern Bridge Conventions* (New York: Crown, 1981), p. 36.

six or more cards in a suit other than opener's, then a weak jump shift (WJS), not 1NT, would be the right bid. WJS bids are preemptive sign offs, showing responder's intolerance for opener's suit but giving the pair a realistic place to play.

Having unlimited non-jump new-suit forcing responses in the system precludes the need for jump shifts to show strong hands and thus allows the partnership to play weak jump shifts, which occur more frequently and are more useful than strong jump shifts. Weak jump shifts are consummately descriptive bids that add another powerful preemptive weapon to your arsenal. Your opponents would surely rather have you playing strong jump shifts.

Here are a few examples of what to respond when partner opens 1♠:

With ♠xx ♥xxx ♦KQxxx ♣xxx, respond 1NT (forcing), then probably pass whatever opener rebids.

With ♠xx ♥Qx ♦Kxxxxx ♣xxx, respond 3♦ (WJS)

With ♠xxx ♥Jx ♦KQxxx ♣xxx, respond 2♠.

With ♠xxx ♥xx ♦KQxxx ♣xxx, pass.

With ♠xx ♥KQx ♦xxxxx ♣KQJ, respond INT (forcing), then probably rebid NT.

With ♠xx ♥xxx ♦KQxxx ♣KQJ, respond 2♦ (forcing), then probably rebid NT.

With ♠xxx ♥xx ♦KQxxx ♣KQJ, respond 2♦ (forcing), then probably rebid spades.

Jacoby 2 No Trump, 3 No Trump, and Splinters

Since there are countless ways to play the Jacoby 2NT system, you and your partner must thoroughly discuss all the possible point counts and distributions, agree upon a coherent and consistent set of responses and rebids, and memorize this whole agreement so that it becomes second nature to both of you before you sit down to play. If you do not understand all the inter-relations of this system — or any bidding system — perfectly, then you should not play it. Play what you know and know what you play.

Rather than go through all the possibilities, I will just describe in detail how I prefer to play the Jacoby 2NT system and mention a few of the reasons why.

First of all, after a major suit opening, the initial response within the Jacoby 2NT system is forcing to game and always shows at least four pieces of trump and the equivalent of a solid opening hand. We are ab-solutely disciplined about these requirements — espe-cially about trump length. The response is unlimited in its HCP and other aspects of strength. Some pairs play that a Jacoby response shows 12-16 or 12-17 HCP, but — why? The response is 100% forcing, so why should it not be unlimited?

Since our side has at least opening hand facing opening hand and a known major suit fit of at least nine cards, there is little to fear from the opponents butting in.

When opener's first rebid is game in the trump suit, it shows minimal values and the desire to play the hand at that level. Responder then becomes cap-tain of the auction and may explore for slam if she wishes. If responder does not have extra values, she should treat this rebid as a sign off. Two principles are at work in this situation: (1) the Principle of Fast Arri-val, which demands that opener bid game directly with a minimum, and (2) the principle that the captaincy belongs to the partner of the first limit bidder.

Three different initial responses show at least four pieces of trump and an opening hand:

2NT shows this hand with no singletons or voids.

3NT shows this hand with an undisclosed singleton.

A splinter bid, i.e., a double jump shift, shows a void in that suit. Responses of 3♠, 4♣, or 4♦ after a 1♥ opening or 4♣, 4♦, or 4♥ after a 1♠ opening are all splinters showing a void in that suit.

After a response of 2NT, if opener has no interest in slam, he shuts the auction off with a direct jump to game, as described above. With extra values, and therefore with interest in slam, opener has three options:

First, with no singletons or voids, opener rebids his original suit at the 3-level. This rebid is a general purpose force, denying shapeliness but implying power. Some pairs reverse the meanings of the 3-level and 4-level original suit rebids, but we see little sense in that strategy. Remember the Principle of Fast Arrival.

Second, with a singleton, opener rebids this suit at the 3-level. On the convention card, "NS3=S" means "New Suit at the 3-Level is a Singleton." Some pairs use this bid to show a real second suit, but our method is superior because (1) a singleton has more playing power than a second suit and (2) knowing length of five or more in opener's major and shortness in this suit, responder can infer opener's likely holding in the other two suits.

Finally, with a void, opener rebids this suit at the 4-level. On the convention card, "NS4=V" means "New Suit at the 4-Level is a Void." Again, *mutatis mutandis*, our method is superior to that of those pairs who use this bid to show *either* a singleton or a void. A void is *much* more powerful than a singleton in the play of the hand, so it is quite worthwhile for opener to tell responder which one he has.

Facing a Jacoby 3NT response and with slam interest, opener bids an artificial 4♣ to ask responder to identify the singleton. If the singleton is in clubs, responder bids the trump suit; otherwise responder just bids the short suit. Without slam interest, opener signs off by bidding game in his suit.

Opposite a splinter response and with slam interest, opener for a rebid starts cue bidding first-round controls up the line.[4] Without slam interest, he signs off in game as described above.

Some responders use splinters to show either a singleton or a void. This is an inadequate employment of what could otherwise be a very helpful tool. The difference between a singleton and a void is important. It could be the difference between bidding or not bidding a small slam, or especially between bidding a small slam or a grand. Here is an example of how such an auction leads to bidding a cold 27-HCP grand slam:

```
Dealer: S          ♠ Q J x x
Vul.: Both         ♥ —
                   ♦ A J x x
                   ♣ Q J T x x

♠ x x x                          ♠ —
♥ A K J          N               ♥ T x x x x x
♦ T x       W    ✧    E          ♦ K Q x x x x
♣ x x x x x      S               ♣ x

                   ♠ A K T x x x
                   ♥ Q x x x
                   ♦ x
                   ♣ A K
```

South	West	North	East
1♠	pass	4♥	pass
5♣	pass	5♦	pass
6♣	pass	6♠	pass
7♠	pass	pass	pass

---

[4] Blackwood is useless with a known void in either hand.

When North bids 6♠, South thinks to himself: "Aha! She has the ♦A but not the ♦K, she's void in hearts, and I have the club honors; therefore she must have a spade honor, probably the ♠Q, for her 11+ HCP to make the splinter response in the first place. So, even if trump split Jxx to none, we can pick them all up with her ♠Q. Thus: 7♠! It should be a laydown at trick five or six."

As indeed it is! Win the club, heart, or spade opening lead. Cash the ♠A, noticing the bad trump split. Ruff a heart. Lead to the ♠K. Ruff a heart. Lead to the ♣A. Pull the last trump, throwing a diamond. Cash the ♣K. Cross to dummy with ♦A. Pitch heart losers under good clubs. Alternately, win the diamond opening lead. Cash the ♠A, noticing the bad trump split. Pull trump. Cash the top clubs. Ruff a heart. Pitch heart losers under good clubs. Note what a key card the ♣T turned out to be!

Well bid!

Short Suit Game Tries, Preemptive Reraises, and Power Tries

A persistent annoyance in the five-card major version of Standard American is the problem of how to open a 16-HCP hand containing a doubleton, two three-card suits, and a five-card major. If we open the major at the 1-level, how do we later show the hand's actual high-card strength? If, conversely, we open 1NT (15-17 HCP), how do we later show the five-card major? Which way are we going to lie to partner?

AWNT solves this problem. By opening 1NT with flat hands of 11½-14 HCP, we gain many new options in the 15-17 HCP range. So, unless the hand demands to be opened 2♣, open all hands containing a five-card major in that major.

To show a flat hand with 15-17 HCP and a five-card major, use the following sequences:

If partner responds 1♠ to your 1♥, jump rebid to 2NT. With a minimum, partner can either pass 2NT or take a preference to 3♥. With a stronger hand, she can either bid game in NT or hearts or begin exploring for slam.

If partner bids 1NT forcing, rebid 2NT, invitational. Again, partner can either pass 2NT, bid 3NT, or take a preference to your major at either the 3-level or the game level.

If partner bids a new suit at the 2-level, rebid 3NT. Partner can either correct to game in your major, if necessary, or begin exploring for slam.

If partner makes a simple raise, rebid 2NT. This shows 15-17 HCP because with 11½-14 you would either pass or rebid 3 of your major, a preemptive reraise (PERR). Partner should treat your 2NT rebid as invitational.

If partner makes a limit raise, rebid 3NT, thus making her the captain and giving her the choice of games.

The 2NT rebids in the above situations and in several others after a major suit opening are called "power tries." They are invitations to game based on sheer HCP strength. Typically they show 16-18 HCP, but could also show a good 15 or a bad 19. The most common sequence involving a power try is: 1♥ or 1♠ - simple raise (6-8 HCP) - 2NT. In Standard American that invitational sequence would be either 1♥ - 2♥ - 3♥ or 1♠ - 2♠ - 3♠, but since AWNT allows us to accomplish this invitation with a 2NT rebid, we prefer to exploit the preemptive value of the 3-level reraise. Opener, knowing after responder's simple raise that game is out of reach, rebids 3 of the major, thus using the preemptive reraise to prevent the opponents from balancing. The opponents, if they are worth their salt, are not going to let us play a suit fit at the 2-level anyway, so we might as well go quickly to the 3-level before they get a chance to exchange any information.

Opener's rebid of any non-jump new suit after responder gives a simple raise shows a short suit —either a singleton or, preferably, a void — and asks responder to bid game in the major if the shortness seems helpful or to shut the auction off at 3 of the major if the shortness seems useless. Like the splinter bid described above, this "short suit game try" (SSGT) takes advantage of the shape and controls in opener's hand to help find a game contract when the side may be deficient in HCP strength.

Dealer: S	♠ Q x x x
Vul.: Both	♥ x x x x x
	♦ A x x
	♣ x

♠ x x		N		♠ J T
♥ K T x	W	♦	E	♥ A Q J x
♦ x x x x		S		♦ J T x
♣ A Q J x				♣ T x x x

♠ A K x x x
♥ x
♦ K Q x
♣ K x x x

South	West	North	East
1♠	pass	2♠	pass
3♥	pass	4♠	pass
pass	pass		

North reasons that even though she is at the bottom of her HCP range, South's singleton or void would cut her heart losers to one or none. She can easily envision a crossruffing line of play in hearts and clubs making the spade game. So she correctly bids 4♠. West can hold North to four by leading a trump; otherwise the contract makes an overtrick.

But what if this were the deal?

```
Dealer: S        ♠ Q x x
Vul.: Both       ♥ A x x
                 ♦ Q x
                 ♣ x x x x x

♠ x x                          ♠ J T x
♥ x x x          N             ♥ J T x x
♦ K T x x x    W ✧ E           ♦ A J x x x
♣ A Q J          S             ♣ T

                 ♠ A K x x x
                 ♥ K Q x
                 ♦ x
                 ♣ K x x x
```

In this case, even with more HCP, North should decline South's 3♦ short suit game try and sign off at 3♠. She can see that South's shortness does not improve her hand. The game goes down, with East-West getting three club tricks and the ♦A.

Funny Raises

The theory behind Bergen raises is for the responder to get the pair as quickly as possible to the proper level of a major suit contract as determined by the Law of

Total Tricks.[5] That is, with exceptions determined by shape and HCP point count, responder holding three trumps bids at the 2-level; holding four, at the 3-level; and holding five, at the 4-level.

Bergen raises are very effective, but rather complicated, too complicated for many of us. Slightly simpler and almost as effective is a system that my partners and I have dubbed "Funny Raises," based on principles derived from Jacoby major raises, limit raises, and modifications of Bergen raises. The general plan of Funny Raises, after a 1-level major suit opening, is:

HCP	Number of trumps	Responder's call
0-4	Zero to four	Pass
5-11	Exactly two	1NT, then single raise
12+	Exactly two	New suit at 2-level
5-8	Exactly three	Single raise
9-11	Exactly three	1NT, then jump raise
12+	Exactly three	3♦
5-8	At least four	3♣
9-11	At least four	Jump raise
12+	At least four (flat)	Jacoby 2NT
12+	At least four (with singleton)	Jacoby 3NT
12+	At least four (with void)	Splinter
0-9	At least five (with singleton or void)	Game raise

On the next page, in ascending order, is the full schedule of Funny Raise responses to the 1♥ opening:

---

[5] Bergen raises are described by Marty Bergen in *Better Bidding with Bergen*, v. 1, *Uncontested Auctions* (Las Vegas: Max Hardy, 1985), pp. 37-43; by Amalya Kearse in *Bridge Conventions Complete* (Louisville: Devyn, 1990), pp. 746-748; and by Magnus Lindkvist in *Bridge: Classic and Modern Conventions*, v. 1 (Bucharest: Arta Grafica, 2001), pp. 97-101.

Pass = 0-4 HCP, no more than four hearts.

1♠ = 5+ HCP, at least four spades, any number of hearts.

1NT = 5-11 HCP, any distribution, no more than three hearts or three spades (standard 1NT forcing).

1NT, then cheapest heart raise = 5-11 HCP (but tends toward lower end of range), exactly two hearts.

1NT, then jump in hearts = 9-11 HCP, exactly three hearts.

2♣ = 12+ HCP, at least four clubs, no more than two hearts (natural, two-over-one game force).

2♦ = 12+ HCP, at least four diamonds, no more than two hearts (natural, two-over-one game force).

2♥ = 5-8 HCP, exactly three hearts (natural).

2♠ = 12+ HCP, at least four spades, no more than two hearts (natural, two-over-one game force, *not* to be treated as a jump shift).

2NT = 12+ HCP, at least four hearts, no singletons or voids (Jacoby raise, artificial, forcing)

3♣ = 5-8 HCP, at least four hearts (artificial, says nothing about clubs, forcing).

3♦ = 12+ HCP, exactly three hearts (artificial, says nothing about diamonds, forcing).

3♥ = 9-11 HCP, at least four hearts (standard limit raise, natural, invitational).

3♠ = 12+ HCP, at least four hearts, void in spades (splinter, forcing).

3NT = 12+ HCP, at least four hearts, undisclosed singleton (opener rebids 4♣ as relay to short suit).

4♣ = 12+ HCP, at least four hearts, void in clubs (splinter, forcing).

4♦ = 12+ HCP, at least four hearts, void in diamonds (splinter, forcing).

4♥ = 0-9 HCP, at least five hearts, undisclosed singleton or void (sign off).

4♠ = 17+ HCP, exactly three hearts (cue bid, shows first-round control of spades, forcing).

4NT = Blackwood, implies 17+ HCP, slam values, no
voids, and either a heart fit or the potential for 6NT.
5♣ = 17+ HCP, exactly three hearts (cue bid, shows
first-round control of clubs, forcing).
5♦ = 17+ HCP, exactly three hearts (cue bid, shows
first-round control of diamonds, forcing).

This schedule may at first seem confusing, arbitrary,
and hard to remember. Here it is for 1♥ in terms of HCP:

If you have:	Then your call is:
0-4 HCP, no more than four hearts	Pass
0-9 HCP, at least five hearts, undisclosed singleton or void	4♥
5-8 HCP, exactly three hearts	2♥
5-8 HCP, at least four hearts	3♣
5-11 HCP, exactly two hearts	1NT, then cheapest raise
5-11 HCP, any distribution, no more than three hearts or three spades	1NT
5+ HCP, at least four spades, any number of hearts	1♠
9-11 HCP, at least four hearts	3♥
9-11 HCP, exactly three hearts	1NT, then jump in hearts
12+ HCP, at least four clubs, no more than two hearts	2♣
12+ HCP, at least four diamonds, no more than two hearts	2♦
12+ HCP, at least four spades, no more than two hearts	2♠
12+ HCP, exactly three hearts	3♦
12+ HCP, at least four hearts, no singletons or voids	2NT
12+ HCP, at least four hearts, undisclosed singleton	3NT
12+ HCP, at least four hearts, club void	4♣

12+ HCP, at least four hearts, diamond void	4♦
12+ HCP, at least four hearts, spade void	3♠
17+ HCP, slam values, no voids	4NT
	(Blackwood)
17+ HCP, exactly three hearts, first-round control of clubs	5♣
17+ HCP, exactly three hearts, first-round control of diamonds	5♦
17+ HCP, exactly three hearts, first-round control of spades	4♠

And here for 1♥ in terms of the number of trumps:

If you have:	Then your call is:
No more than two hearts, 12+ HCP, at least four clubs	2♣
No more than two hearts, 12+ HCP, at least four diamonds	2♦
No more than two hearts, 12+ HCP, at least four spades	2♠
Exactly two hearts, 5-11 HCP	1NT, then cheapest raise
No more than three hearts or three spades, any distribution, 5-11 HCP	1NT
Exactly three hearts, 5-8 HCP	2♥
Exactly three hearts, 9-11 HCP	1NT, then jump in hearts
Exactly three hearts, 12+ HCP	3♦
Exactly three hearts, 17+ HCP, first-round control of clubs	5♣
Exactly three hearts, 17+ HCP, first-round control of diamonds	5♦
Exactly three hearts, 17+ HCP, first-round control of spades	4♠
No more than four hearts, 0-4 HCP	pass
At least four hearts, 5-8 HCP	3♣
At least four hearts, 9-11 HCP	3♥

At least four hearts, no singletons or voids, 12+ HCP	2NT
At least four hearts, undisclosed singleton, 12+ HCP	3NT
At least four hearts, club void, 12+ HCP	4♣
At least four hearts, diamond void, 12+ HCP	4♦
At least four hearts, spade void, 12+ HCP	3♠
At least five hearts, 0-9 HCP, undisclosed singleton or void	4♥
Any number of hearts, at least four spades, 5+ HCP	1♠
Any number of hearts, 17+ HCP, slam values, no voids	4NT (Blackwood)

Here, following the same principles, is the complete schedule of Funny Raise responses to the 1♠ opening:

Pass = 0-4 HCP, no more than four spades.

1NT = 5-11 HCP, any distribution, no more than four hearts or three spades (standard 1NT forcing).

1NT, then cheapest spade raise = 5-11 HCP (but tends toward lower end of range), exactly two spades.

1NT, then jump in spades = 9-11 HCP, exactly three spades.

2♣ = 12+ HCP, at least four clubs, no more than two spades (natural, two-over-one game force).

2♦ = 12+ HCP, at least four diamonds, no more than two spades (natural, two-over-one game force).

2♥ = 12+ HCP, at least five hearts, no more than two spades (natural, two-over-one game force).

2♠ = 5-8 HCP, exactly three spades (natural).

2NT = 12+ HCP, at least four spades, no singletons or voids (Jacoby raise, artificial, forcing)

3♣ = 5-8 HCP, at least four spades (artificial, says nothing about clubs, forcing).

3♦ = 12+ HCP, exactly three spades (artificial, says nothing about diamonds, forcing).

3♥ = 0-7 HCP, at least six hearts, no more than one spade (standard WJS).

3♠ = 9-11 HCP, at least four spades (standard limit raise, natural, invitational).

3NT = 12+ HCP, at least four spades, undisclosed singleton (opener rebids 4♣ as relay to short suit).

4♣ = 12+ HCP, at least four spades, void in clubs (splinter, forcing).

4♦ = 12+ HCP, at least four spades, void in diamonds (splinter, forcing).

4♥ = 12+ HCP, at least four spades, void in hearts (splinter, forcing).

4♠ = 0-9 HCP, at least five spades, undisclosed singleton or void (sign off).

4NT = Blackwood, implies 17+ HCP, slam values, no voids, and either a spade fit or the potential for 6NT.

5♣ = 17+ HCP, exactly three spades (cue bid, shows first-round control of clubs, forcing).

5♦ = 17+ HCP, exactly three spades (cue bid, shows first-round control of diamonds, forcing).

5♥ = 17+ HCP, exactly three spades (cue bid, shows first-round control of hearts, forcing).

Here it is for 1♠ in terms of HCP:

If you have:	Then your call is:
0-4 HCP, no more than four spades	Pass
0-7 HCP, at least six hearts, no more than one spade	3♥
0-9 HCP, at least five spades, undisclosed singleton or void	4♠
5-8 HCP, exactly three spades	2♠
5-8 HCP, at least four spades	3♣
5-11 HCP, exactly two spades	1NT, then cheapest raise
5-11 HCP, any distribution, no more than four hearts or three spades	1NT

9-11 HCP, at least four spades	3♠
9-11 HCP, exactly three spades	1NT,
	then jump in spades
12+ HCP, at least four clubs, no more than two spades	2♣
12+ HCP, at least four diamonds, no more than two spades	2♦
12+ HCP, at least five hearts, no more than two spades	2♥
12+ HCP, exactly three spades	3♦
12+ HCP, at least four spades, no singletons or voids	2NT
12+ HCP, at least four spades, undisclosed singleton	3NT
12+ HCP, at least four spades, club void	4♣
12+ HCP, at least four spades, diamond void	4♦
12+ HCP, at least four spades, heart void	4♥
17+ HCP, slam values, no voids	4NT
	(Blackwood)
17+ HCP, exactly three spades, first-round control of clubs	5♣
17+ HCP, exactly three spades, first-round control of diamonds	5♦
17+ HCP, exactly three spades, first-round control of hearts	5♥

Again for 1♠ in terms of the number of trumps:

If you have:	Then your call is:
No more than one spade, at least six hearts, 0-7 HCP	3♥
No more than two spades, 12+ HCP, at least four clubs	2♣
No more than two spades, 12+ HCP, at least four diamonds	2♦
No more than two spades, 12+ HCP, at least five hearts	2♥

Exactly two spades, 5-11 HCP	1NT,
	then cheapest raise
No more than three spades or four hearts, any distribution, 5-11 HCP	1NT
Exactly three spades, 5-8 HCP	2♠
Exactly three spades, 9-11 HCP	1NT,
	then jump in spades
Exactly three spades, 12+ HCP	3♦
Exactly three spades, 17+ HCP, first-round control of clubs	5♣
Exactly three spades, 17+ HCP, first-round control of diamonds	5♦
Exactly three spades, 17+ HCP, first-round control of hearts	5♥
No more than four spades, 0-4 HCP	pass
At least four spades, 5-8 HCP	3♣
At least four spades, 9-11 HCP	3♠
At least four spades, no singletons or voids, 12+ HCP	2NT
At least four spades, undisclosed singleton, 12+ HCP	3NT
At least four spades, club void, 12+ HCP	4♣
At least four spades, diamond void, 12+ HCP	4♦
At least four spades, heart void, 12+ HCP	4♥
At least five spades, 0-9 HCP, undisclosed singleton or void	4♠
Any number of spades, 17+ HCP, slam values, no voids	4NT (Blackwood)

With the one exception of the 1♠ - 3♥ sequence, you cannot play weak jump shifts in conjunction with Funny Raises. There are always trade-offs. If you really like WJS, don't play Funny Raises. In any case, you can still play WJS after a minor suit opening.

3

Minor Suit Openings

When we either open a NT in the first round of bidding or show a NT hand by a prescribed sequence in the second round, when we respond a natural NT, or when we open or respond a major, we are aiming to play the contract in that strain. Not so with the minors. Not at all so! Whenever we open a minor we are immediately looking to get out of it into either NT or a major — unless a minor suit slam is possible. The reason that we have such contempt for the minors is mathematical: They pay off less. Game in a minor is worth either 400 or 600, the same as game in NT, but 3NT requires taking only nine tricks while 5♣ or 5♦ requires taking eleven. Moreover, an overtrick at 3NT — a common occurrence — is worth 430 or 630, but an overtrick at 5♣ or 5♦ — a rare occurrence — is worth only 420 or 620. This is a disaster at matchpoints and means that *you should have bid 6*. Minor suit games are incredibly hard to make and hardly worth the effort. Whenever you consider bidding a minor suit game, ask yourself: "Why am I not bidding either 3NT or slam?" Then bid 5♣ or 5♦ only when 3NT, 6♣, or 6♦ seems impossible.

Opposite a 1♣ or 1♦ opening, responder's first obligation — her absolute duty — is to show a four-card or longer major if she has one. With both four-card majors, she bids up the line, giving opener the chance to bid spades and thus reveal their four-four spade fit. With five or more hearts and four spades, she bids hearts first, giving opener the chance to show spades on the 1-level. At that point opener's absolute duty is to rebid spades if he has four. With five or more spades and either four or five hearts, she bids spades first — unless she is planning to reverse — giving opener the chance to bid hearts on the 2-level. Again, at that point opener's absolute duty is to rebid hearts if he has four. All her responses are unlimited and forcing, in keeping with the precept that any new suit bid by an unpassed responder is forcing.

All these unlimited, forcing major suit responses are made at the 1-level. Responding in a major at the 2-level is a weak jump shift (a shut-off bid); responding in a major at the 3-level is a splinter, showing a singleton or a void in that major, extraordinary support for opener's minimum three-card minor, and slam interest; and responding in a major at the 4-level is weak, preemptive, and to play.

To respond to an opening 1♣ or 1♦ with anything other than a major — in an uncontested auction — is to deny having as many as three cards in either major.

The contempt that we have for the minors in general is exceeded only by the contempt that responder should have for diamonds. Even with a hand like this, ♠— ♥xxxx ♦AKQxxxxxx ♣—, responder should bypass diamonds in the first round of bidding and bid the major. After she has introduced the major into the auction, she can bid diamonds freely in every round thereafter. Opener will get the message.

The graduated NT responses to 1♣ or 1♦ are: 1NT showing 6-9 HCP, 2NT showing 10-12 HCP, and 3NT showing 13-15 HCP. There are many other frequently encountered ranges for these three bids. Among the most popular are: 6-10, 11-12, and 13-15. But 6-10 HCP is too wide and 11-12 is too narrow. Since these responses are limit bids, responder wants to give the new captain of the auction as much useful information as possible. Some of the most useful information that the captain can receive in almost any auction is the range of partner's strength, accurate to within one trick. There is more than one trick's worth of difference between 6 HCP and 10 HCP.

Note that the 1NT, 6-9 HCP response to 1♣ shows precisely 3♠-3♥-3♦-4♣ shape. If responder had four or more in either major, she would bid the major. If she had five clubs, she would bid it at the 3-level as an inverted minor. If she had four or more diamonds, she would prefer to bid diamonds rather than 1NT to try to get the stronger hand to become declarer at NT. Conversely, the 1NT, 6-9 HCP response to 1♦ can show a variety of shapes from 3♠-3♥-3♦-4♣ or 3♠-3♥-4♦-3♣ to 2♠-2♥-4♦-5♣ or even 1♠-3♥-4♦-5♣ or 3♠-1♥-4♦-5♣. With five or more diamonds, responder would bid an inverted minor. With six or more clubs, she would likely make a weak jump shift.

When the 1♣ or 1♦ opening is overcalled with a suit at the 1-level so that all three NT responses remain available, the usual ranges of 6-9, 10-12, and 13-15 HCP still apply, but, as with all NT responses in a competitive auction, stoppers must now be taken into account. Moreover, hands with exactly four cards in a major, i.e., hands that would have required a major suit response in an uncontested auction — compliant with responder's first duty — now become eligible for a NT bid as a response, since to respond with a major directly when opener has been overcalled would show five or more cards in that major. It is more important to show the four-card major than the stopper. A negative double is preferable to show that four-card major, but a negative double is not always possible.

With a stopper in RHO's suit, and usually without a four-card major, bid your appropriate NT response just as though RHO had passed. For this purpose, any holding in RHO's suit as strong as 9xxx or better is regarded as a stopper. Without a stopper in RHO's suit, do not bid any kind of NT. Either bid your other minor if it is four cards or longer or, if you have a four-card major, consider a negative double.

When partner opens a minor and RHO overcalls the other minor, your negative double, made with at least 6 HCP at the 1-level or with at least 10 HCP at the 2-level, promises four-three or four-four length in the majors, ideally four-four. With weaker hands, three-five, four-five, or five-five shape in the majors are also possible.

When partner opens a minor and RHO overcalls a major, your negative double promises at least four cards in the other major, but says nothing about the other minor. With at least 6 HCP at the 1-level or at least 10 HCP at the 2-level, the negative double promises exactly four cards in your major. With weaker hands you may hold five for your negative double. With six or more you would make a preemptive jump shift.

These promises are absolute. Partner must be able to depend on your announced length and shape.

When partner opens a minor, RHO overcalls a suit, and you respond some level of NT, partner will realize that you may have one four-card major and no more than two cards in the other. Partner should then rebid his cheapest four-card major, if he has one, thus giving you the chance either to raise his major or bid your own.

There are four situations in which we should open 1 of a minor:

1. Starting a sequence to show the equivalent of a Standard American 1NT opener, i.e., 15-17 HCP balanced. We will discuss this in detail in Chapter 4.

When responding to an opening 1♣ or 1♦, remember during the first round of the auction that partner's bid could turn out to show a strong, balanced NT hand — and plan accordingly.

2. Starting a sequence to show a flat 18-19 HCP NT hand. This is also a topic of Chapter 4. Again, responder should bear in mind that this apparently minor-suit opening may really be a NT opening.

3. Starting a sequence to show a four-card major in a hand with no five-card or longer major.

4. Starting a sequence to show a hand that really has a five-card or longer minor.

In the third situation, if responder bids either a minor or NT, thereby denying a four-card or longer major, then it might seem futile for opener to rebid his major. There is, after all, as both partners now know, no four-four major fit to be found. Nevertheless, without NT shape, opener should still rebid the major as he originally intended. Responder will then know that opener has exactly four cards in that major as well as some imbalance which prevents him from bidding NT.

Also in the third situation, if responder bids a major, opener's first obligation now becomes to support responder's major if possible. With four-card support, opener must rebid responder's major. A single raise shows 15-17 playing points (sometimes shaded down to 14 or 13); a jump raise short of game shows 22+ playing points and suggests slam interest; and a raise to game shows 19-21 playing points.

You might ask: How would opener rebid to show an imbalanced 11-point hand with four-card support for responder's major? The answer is: There is no such problem, because there is no such hand. Any 11-HCP hand that could not be opened 1NT but still could be opened, and that contains a four-card major, naturally contains enough distribution points — counting a void as 5, a singleton as 3, and a doubleton as 1 — to bring its total of playing points up to at least 13,[1] and almost always more than that.

In the fourth situation, rebid the minor, thereby denying both NT shape and a four-card major. With 16+ HCP, jump in the minor.

In both the third and fourth situations, opener's hand is usually not balanced. If it were, opener would have bid either 1NT (11½-14 HCP) or 2NT (20-21 HCP) directly or used a NT-showing sequence such as in situations one or two above. Even when the minor-suit opener holds three cards in responder's major or four cards in the other major — or four cards in both majors if responder has bid a minor — he should rebid NT when he has NT shape. The responder who has bid a major can use Checkback Stayman (another topic of Chapter 4) to find that major in opener's hand.

With equal length in the minors — unless you are planning to reverse — usually open 1♦, regardless of suit quality. Even holdings such as ♦xxxx ♣AKQJ should be opened 1♦. With unequal length always open the longer minor. This consistency helps to give responder, who may well become the captain of the auction, a clearer picture of your hand.

Minor openings in AWNT always show at least three cards. We do not play the short club. Because opener could have as few as three, always have at least five pieces when raising a minor. We want to avoid Moysian fits whenever possible.

Raising a minor takes two forms. A jump raise is weak, preemptive, and to play, showing 0-8 HCP, five or more pieces of trump, and no four-card or longer major. A single raise also indicates five or more pieces of trump and no four-card or longer major, but is constructive, forcing, and should show 12+ HCP or the

---

[1] This 11-HCP, 13-playing-point opening hand would have exactly 4♠-2♥-2♦-5♣, 4♠-2♥-5♦-2♣, 2♠-4♥-2♦-5♣, or 2♠-4♥-5♦-2♣ shape. It is the weakest possible support hand for responder's major.

equivalent in playing points. With an in-between raising hand, i.e., five or more pieces, no four-card or longer major, and 9-11 HCP, responder can make a temporizing bid in the other minor if it is at least four cards or, barring that, bid NT. This system of minor suit raises, "inverted minors," has become quite popular in Standard American as well as K-S.

In a competitive auction, inverted minors remain in effect if and only if both responses remain available. That is, if 1♦, for instance, is overcalled with 1♥, 1♠, 1NT, or 1♣, then a response of 2♦ is still an inverted minor forcing raise and a response of 3♦ is still an inverted minor preemptive raise. If the overcall is 2♦ or higher, then the forcing raise is off but the preemptive raise remains possible. If responder wishes to force opener, she can either bid a new suit at the cheapest level or cue bid the enemy suit.

One flaw — perhaps the greatest flaw — of the K-S system is the sequence where opener bids 1 of a minor, responder bids 1 of a major, and opener raises responder's major. This sequence shows 15-17 playing points and precisely four pieces of trump in opener's hand for that major. Examples of opener's hand might be, when opener bids 1♦ and responder's major is hearts:

♠xx ♥AQxx ♦Axxx ♣AJx

♠AJxx ♥KQxx ♦xxxxx ♣—

♠— ♥Axxx ♦KQxxxxx ♣xx

♠A ♥xxxx ♦Kxxx ♣KQxx

♠AKQJ ♥xxxx ♦xxx ♣Ax

All these examples show 15 playing points, one just in HCP, and the others counting distribution as 5 for a void, 3 for a singleton, and 1 for a doubleton.

Note how very unlikely it is that this sequence would ever show opener holding less than 15-point support for responder's major, because, with less than 15 playing points in either major, opener would usually open 1NT in our system.

The flaw is that, with this sequence, the weaker hand almost always becomes declarer. The only exception would be when responder has slam-going values. Having a major suit contract played from the wrong side of the table is not as dangerous as having a NT contract played from the wrong side, but it is still undesirable. We might invent some elaborate mechanism to transfer such contracts to the strong hand, i.e., opener's hand, but that sequence would probably be too complicated to be workable.

4

No Trump
Openings

In standard bidding you open 1NT to show a strong flat hand, but open 1 of a minor and rebid the cheapest NT to show a weak flat hand. In K-S bidding these meanings are reversed. This is the pivot of the entire K-S system and all the other systems that are derived from it. Therefore this chapter and the next are the core of this book.

To show the various opening NT ranges in the AWNT system, we use the following schedule:

11½-14 HCP: Open 1NT.

15-17 HCP: Open 1♣ or 1♦ and, in an uncontested auction, rebid 1NT. In a competitive auction there are nuances that will be described below.

18-19 HCP: Open 1♣ or 1♦ and rebid 2NT.

20-21 HCP: Open 2NT.

22-23 HCP: Open 2♣ and rebid 2NT.

24-25 HCP: Open 2♣ and rebid 3NT.

26+ HCP: Open 2♣, evaluate partner's hand, and play it by ear. If partner has any values at all, and if there is a good fit, slam is likely.

If you do not play the gambling 3NT opening, you can open 3NT to show 26-27 HCP, and then use the 2♣ "play it by ear" opening to show 28+ HCP.

For all of these openings, do not worry about having stoppers if your hand is acceptably flat. I have absolutely no qualms about opening 2NT with a small doubleton. But pay strict attention to shape. Your hand should be no shapelier than 2-3-3-5, 2-2-4-5 or — rarely — 2-2-3-6 and should *never* — unless you are playing puppet Stayman or some similar compensating device — contain a five-card major.[1]

You can get away with a lot in K-S, but you still must — most of the time — remember which bidding system you are using! Here's a funny story:

When I started to learn K-S, several of my partners and I were learning it together. One night we were playing K-S — or so we thought. I had a flat 12-count which I opened 1♦. My partner had a flat 14-count. He responded 1♠. Since I had only two spades, I rebid 1NT. Partner naturally thought I had 15-17 HCP in a balanced hand. Since he had two aces and good spots, he decided to risk a quantitative 4NT. I thought he must have at least 18 HCP to bid Blackwood opposite my 12-14 HCP. I showed him my two aces. He hesitated briefly then bid 6NT.

When dummy came down I was shocked. I was expecting 18 or more HCP and it looked like down two. Then all of a sudden it dawned on me what I had done: showing my weak NT hand with a Standard American sequence that meant strong NT in K-S. I stammered, "Sorry, partner, I misbid," even before I played to the first trick. But every finesse worked! Every other pair in the room had bid correctly and was in 3NT making

---

[1] Potential NT hands with semi-flat shape (2-2-4-5 or 2-2-3-6) demand that more attention be paid to their stoppers. Tend to open them as NT hands only if both short suits are stopped and the long suit is runnable, e.g., ♠Ax ♥Qxx ♦Kx ♣AKJxxx.

six for 690. But we alone, who had bid wrong, were in 6NT making six for 1440, a cold top!

I would not, however, recommend that method for consistently achieving top boards! The game is better served and the other pairs remain more amicable when you earn what you get. But crushing them with my own stupidity sure was fun just that once!

Why the Weak No Trump?

There are at least three good reasons why the K-S system of NT openings makes AWNT superior to Standard American:

1. K-S NT openings in all ranges are more descriptive and versatile as limit bids than in Standard American, thus giving partner more information.
2. Because you will be dealt an 11½-14 HCP hand about 26% of the time, but a 15-17 HCP hand only about 10% of the time, direct 1NT openings occur more often in K-S than in Standard American. This increased frequency of 1NT openings has a very disruptive influence on the opponents of K-S players, since they can generally cope much easier with a Standard American opening of 1 of a minor leading toward a rebid of 1NT than with an immediate K-S opening of 1NT, which forces them to begin their auction at the 2-level.
3. K-S 1NT openings have a preemptive dimension that Standard American 1NT openings simply do not. When you open a 15-17 HCP NT, there are only 23-25 HCP left in the deck. This means that the opponents on average have about 15½-17 between them. But when you open an 11½-14 HCP NT, there

are 26-28½ HCP left, giving the opponents together on average about 17½-19. In other words, chances are, when you open a strong NT, they would be out of the auction anyway; but when you open a weak NT, you may actually be keeping them out.

Responses to the 11½-14 HCP No Trump Opening Hand

"11½" means "a good 11." That is, the hand should have an ace or a protected king or solid honors in one suit and usually at least 1½ quick tricks. *Do not be shy!* Interpret this requirement liberally. Remember to exploit the preemptive dimension of the K-S 1NT hand. When in doubt, open it!

When responding on the 2-level in an uncontested auction to partner's opening weak 1NT, whether or not you are a passed hand makes quite a bit of difference.

The theory behind Jacoby transfers is that the stronger of the two hands on offense should remain concealed as declarer. When playing 15-17 HCP NT openings, Jacoby transfers, especially for the majors, always make sense. But if the opening NT is only 11½-14 HCP, then Jacoby transfers are not so important. With strong NT openings, responder's hand is almost certain to be weaker than opener's; but with weak NT openings, there is no such expectation. Responder may often be as strong as or stronger than opener. However, if responder is a passed hand, then everyone at the table knows that responder's hand is weaker than opener's. Therefore, we play that Jacoby transfers are on after a weak 1NT opening only if responder is a passed hand. This arrangement frees the 2♦ response for a very important purpose when responder is an unpassed hand — Forcing Stayman.

In Standard American, playing Jacoby transfers, we cannot distinguish between degrees of Stayman, but in AWNT, we can use 2♣ by either a passed or an unpassed hand as non-forcing Stayman and 2♦ by an unpassed hand as forcing Stayman. Non-forcing Stayman is just the plain old Stayman that we all know, except that now it has an upper strength limit of about 10 or a bad 11 HCP. Forcing Stayman therefore shows 11+ HCP and will typically lead to game unless an extraordinary misfit comes to light.

Since the weak 1NT opening hand is severely limited and in many ways at the mercy of the opponents,[2] responder must have plenty of "drop dead" suit bids available. For example, all Jacoby transfers opposite a weak 1NT opening, even those that might be made by an unpassed hand, would be drop dead signals. If responder wants opener to become declarer in a major suit game, she must use a Texas transfer.

Hence the full schedule of responses to the K-S weak 1NT opening is:

Pass = Either tolerance for 1NT or inability to rescue

2♣ = Non-forcing Stayman; could be "Garbage Stayman," showing a weak three-suiter with short clubs

2♦ by unpassed hand (BUPH) = Forcing (usually game-forcing) Stayman; all-purpose force, promises only three or more cards in a major; possible slam interest.

2♦ by passed hand (BPH) = Drop dead Jacoby transfer to 2♥

2♥ BUPH = Drop dead; five or more hearts, 0-7 HCP

2♥ BPH = Drop dead Jacoby transfer to 2♠

---

[2] For a full discussion of how to escape when your opening 1NT puts your side in danger, see Chapter 5.

2♠ BUPH = Drop dead; five or more spades, 0-7 HCP

2♠ BPH = Drop dead minor suit Stayman (MSS), ordering opener to run out to a minor to play at the 3-level

2NT = Invitation to 3NT; 11 HCP balanced, no four-card major

3♣ = Drop dead; five or more clubs, 0-7 HCP

3♦ = Drop dead; five or more diamonds, 0-7 HCP

3♥ = Game force to either 3NT or 4♥; at least five hearts and usually 13+ HCP; possible slam interest

3♠ = Game force to either 3NT or 4♠; at least five spades and usually 13+ HCP; possible slam interest

3NT = Drop dead; 12-17 HCP balanced with no four-card major

4♣ = Gerber

4♦ = Texas transfer to 4♥

4♥ = Texas transfer to 4♠

4♠ = Game-forcing MSS with possible slam interest.

4NT = Good 18 to bad 20 HCP, standard quantitative raise, invites to 6NT

5♣ = Strong or highly distributional one-suited club hand, but missing AK of trump; invitation to slam; opener should pass with neither club honor or bid 6♣ with one or both

5♦ = Strong or highly distributional one-suited diamond hand, but missing AK of trump; invitation to slam; opener should pass with neither diamond honor or bid 6♦ with one or both

5♥ = Strong or highly distributional one-suited heart hand, but missing AK of trump; invitation to slam; opener should pass with neither heart honor or bid 6♥ with one or both

5♠ = Strong or highly distributional one-suited spade hand, but missing AK of trump; invitation to slam; opener should pass with neither honor or bid 6♠ with one or both

5NT = Grand slam force; 23-24 HCP; opener should bid 6NT with a minimum or 7NT with a maximum

6♣ = Drop dead; strong or highly distributional one-suited club hand

6♦ = Drop dead; strong or highly distributional one-suited diamond hand

6♥ = Drop dead; strong or highly distributional one-suited heart hand

6♠ = Drop dead; strong or highly distributional one-suited spade hand

6NT = Drop dead; 21-22 HCP

7♣ = Responder able to count at least twelve tricks in her own hand with clubs as trump

7♦ = Responder able to count at least twelve tricks in her own hand with diamonds as trump

7♥ = Responder able to count at least twelve tricks in her own hand with hearts as trump

7♠ = Responder able to count at least twelve tricks in her own hand with spades as trump

7NT = 25-29 HCP and at least three aces.

Responses to the 15-17 HCP No Trump Opening Hand

We show the 15-17 HCP balanced hand by opening 1 of a minor then rebidding 1NT. This rebid does not deny a four-card major, even if partner has bid it, as is explained in the section below on "Checkback Stayman." After opener's 1NT rebid, the responses in an uncontested auction follow the same general pattern as above, except that the "passed hand vs. unpassed hand" restriction that we use with the weak NT disappears in the case of the strong NT and many of the "drop dead" restrictions no longer apply. The full schedule of responder's rebids after 1♣/♦ - 1♦/♥/♠ - 1NT is:

Pass = 0-5 HCP, usually flat.

2♣ = Stayman; could be "Garbage Stayman," showing a weak three-suiter with short clubs

2♦ = Jacoby transfer to 2♥ (or to 3♥ with superacceptance)

2♥ = Jacoby transfer to 2♠ (or to 3♠ with superacceptance)

2♠ = MSS, requiring opener to bid his better minor or 2NT with equal length in the minors (i.e., either three-three or four-four); may show slam interest

2NT = Invitation to 3NT; 8 HCP balanced, no four-card major

3♣ = Drop dead; five or more clubs, 0-6 HCP

3♦ = Drop dead; five or more diamonds, 0-6 HCP

3♥ = Game force to either 3NT or 4♥; at least five hearts and usually 10+ HCP; possible slam interest

3♠ = Game force to either 3NT or 4♠; at least five spades and usually 10+ HCP; possible slam interest

3NT = Drop dead; 9-15 HCP balanced with no four-card major

4♣ = Gerber

4♦ = Texas transfer to 4♥

4♥ = Texas transfer to 4♠

4♠ = Game-forcing MSS with no slam interest; tends to show weak two-suited hand inappropriate as dummy at 3NT

4NT = 16 to 17 HCP, standard quantitative raise, invites to 6NT

5♣ = Strong or highly distributional one-suited club hand, but missing AK of trump; invitation to slam; opener should pass with neither club honor or bid 6♣ with one or both

5♦ = Strong or highly distributional one-suited diamond hand, but missing AK of trump; invitation to slam; opener should pass with neither diamond honor or bid 6♦ with one or both

5♥ = Strong or highly distributional one-suited heart hand, but missing AK of trump; invitation to slam;

opener should pass with neither heart honor or bid
6♥ with one or both

5♠ = Strong or highly distributional one-suited spade
hand, but missing AK of trump; invitation to slam;
opener should pass with neither honor or bid 6♠
with one or both

5NT = Grand slam force; 20-21 HCP; opener should
bid 6NT with a minimum or 7NT with a maximum

6♣ = Drop dead; strong or highly distributional one-
suited club hand

6♦ = Drop dead; strong or highly distributional one-
suited diamond hand

6♥ = Drop dead; strong or highly distributional one-
suited heart hand

6♠ = Drop dead; strong or highly distributional one-
suited spade hand

6NT = Drop dead; 18-19 HCP

7♣ = Responder able to count at least ten tricks in
her own hand with clubs as trump

7♦ = Responder able to count at least ten tricks in her
own hand with diamonds as trump

7♥ = Responder able to count at least ten tricks in her
own hand with hearts as trump

7♠ = Responder able to count at least ten tricks in her
own hand with spades as trump

7NT= 22-25 HCP

Responses to the 18-19 HCP No Trump Opening Hand

The strong balanced 18-19 HCP hand is shown in
AWNT exactly as it is shown in Standard American: by
opening 1 of a minor, then, in an uncontested auction,

jumping to the cheapest level of NT, usually 2NT, but possibly 3NT if responder bids a suit at the 2-level. Responder's rebids after opener's 2NT rebid are:

Pass = 0-4 HCP, usually flat

3♣ = Stayman; could be "Garbage Stayman," showing a weak three-suiter with short clubs

3♦ = Jacoby transfer to 3♥

3♥ = Jacoby transfer to 3♠

3♠ = MSS, requiring opener to bid his better minor or 2NT with equal length in the minors (i.e., either three-three or four-four); may show slam interest

3NT = Drop dead; 6-11 HCP balanced with no four-card major

4♣ = Gerber

4♦ = Texas transfer to 4♥

4♥ = Texas transfer to 4♠

4♠ = Game-forcing MSS with no slam interest; tends to show weak two-suited hand inappropriate as dummy at 3NT

4NT = 14 HCP, standard quantitative raise, invites to 6NT

5♣ = Strong or highly distributional one-suited club hand, but missing AK of trump; invitation to slam; opener should pass with neither club honor or bid 6♣ with one or both

5♦ = Strong or highly distributional one-suited diamond hand, but missing AK of trump; invitation to slam; opener should pass with neither diamond honor or bid 6♦ with one or both

5♥ = Strong or highly distributional one-suited heart hand, but missing AK of trump; invitation to slam; opener should pass with neither heart honor or bid 6♥ with one or both

5♠ = Strong or highly distributional one-suited spade hand, but missing AK of trump; invitation to slam; opener should pass with neither honor or bid 6♠ with one or both

5NT = Grand slam force; 18-19 HCP; opener should bid 6NT with a minimum or 7NT with a maximum

6♣ = Drop dead; strong or highly distributional one-suited club hand

6♦ = Drop dead; strong or highly distributional one-suited diamond hand

6♥ = Drop dead; strong or highly distributional one-suited heart hand

6♠ = Drop dead; strong or highly distributional one-suited spade hand

6NT = Drop dead; 16-17 HCP

7♣ = Responder able to count at least nine tricks in her own hand with clubs as trump

7♦ = Responder able to count at least nine tricks in her own hand with diamonds as trump

7♥ = Responder able to count at least nine tricks in her own hand with hearts as trump

7♠ = Responder able to count at least nine tricks in her own hand with spades as trump

7NT = 20-22 HCP

Responses to the 20-21 HCP No Trump Opening

After a strong 2NT opening of 20-21 HCP, balanced, no singletons or voids, no more than one doubleton, but possibly with a five-card major, the responses are:

Pass = 0-3 HCP, no five-card major

3♣ = Puppet Stayman (responder has no five-card major and no void)

3♦ = Jacoby transfer to 3♥

3♥ = Jacoby transfer to 3♠

3♠ = ConFit

3NT = 4-9 HCP balanced, ends the auction

4♣ = Gerber

4♦ = Texas transfer to 4♥

4♥ = Texas transfer to 4♠

4♠ = MSS

4NT = 11-12 HCP, standard quantitative raise, invites to 6NT

5♣ = Void in clubs with 4♠-4♥-5♦-0♣ distribution; slam-going values

5♦ = Void in diamonds with 4♠-4♥-0♦-5♣ distribution; slam-going values

5♥ = Void in hearts with 4♠-0♥-5♦-4♣ or 4♠-0♥-4♦-5♣ distribution; slam-going values

5♠ = Void in spades with 0♠-4♥-5♦-4♣ or 0♠-4♥-4♦-5♣ distribution; slam-going values

5NT = Grand slam force; 16-17 HCP; opener should bid 6NT with a minimum or 7NT with a maximum

6♣ = 11-12 HCP, quantitative raise with help in clubs, invites to 6NT, but opener should feel confident to pass clubs

6♦ = 11-12 HCP, quantitative raise with help in diamonds, invites to 6NT, but opener should feel confident to pass diamonds

6♥ = 11-12 HCP, quantitative raise with help in hearts, invites to 6NT, but opener should feel confident to pass hearts

6♠ = 11-12 HCP, quantitative raise with help in spades, invites to 6NT, but opener should feel confident to pass spades

6NT = 13-14 HCP balanced, ends the auction.

7♣ = Responder able to count at least eight tricks in her own hand with clubs as trump

7♦ = Responder able to count at least eight tricks in her own hand with diamonds as trump

7♥ = Responder able to count at least eight tricks in her own hand with hearts as trump

7♠ = Responder able to count at least eight tricks in her own hand with spades as trump

7NT = 18-20 HCP.

One of the most difficult decisions in bridge is whether to raise opener's 2NT to game with 4 HCP, or a good 3, or even a bad 5. On the one hand, we always want to be in game with a combined 24 HCP. On the other hand, big hands opposite near-zero hands just do not play very well at 3NT. So, even though 21 + 3 = 24, responder should pass with 3 HCP but bid 3NT with 4. Unfortunately there is not enough room to insert an invitation.

Another problem with the strong 2NT opening is: How can responder show a long minor possibly leading to a minor suit slam? There seems to be little chance of accomplishing this unless we either use 5♣ and 5♦ as natural slam-invitational bids or forget about Confit and use 3♠ as MSS, thus giving us adequate bidding space to explore the minors.

Responses to the 22-23 and 24-25 HCP No Trump Openings

These ranges are shown by opening a strong, artificial, and forcing 2♣ then rebidding either 2NT for 22-23 HCP or 3NT for 24-25 HCP. The respective sets of responses are:

Pass = 0-1 HCP, no five-card major
3♣ = Puppet Stayman (responder has no five-card major and no void)
3♦ = Jacoby transfer to 3♥
3♥ = Jacoby transfer to 3♠
3♠ = ConFit
3NT = 2-7 HCP balanced, ends the auction
4♣ = Gerber
4♦ = Texas transfer to 4♥

4♥ = Texas transfer to 4♠

4♠ = MSS

4NT = 9-10 HCP, standard quantitative raise, invites
to 6NT

5♣ = Void in clubs with 4♠-4♥-5♦-0♣ distribution;
slam-going values

5♦ = Void in diamonds with 4♠-4♥-0♦-5♣ distribution;
slam-going values

5♥ = Void in hearts with 4♠-0♥-5♦-4♣ or 4♠-0♥-4♦-5♣
distribution; slam-going values

5♠ = Void in spades with 0♠-4♥-5♦-4♣ or 0♠-4♥-4♦-5♣
distribution; slam-going values

5NT = Grand slam force; 14-15 HCP; opener should
bid 6NT with a minimum or 7NT with a maximum

6♣ = 9-10 HCP, quantitative raise with help in clubs,
invites to 6NT, but opener should feel confident to
pass clubs

6♦ = 9-10 HCP, quantitative raise with help in diamonds, invites to 6NT, but opener should feel confident to pass diamonds

6♥ = 9-10 HCP, quantitative raise with help in hearts,
invites to 6NT, but opener should feel confident to
pass hearts

6♠ = 9-10 HCP, quantitative raise with help in spades,
invites to 6NT, but opener should feel confident to
pass spades

6NT = 11-12 HCP balanced, ends the auction.

7♣ = Responder able to count at least seven tricks in
her own hand with clubs as trump

7♦ = Responder able to count at least seven tricks in
her own hand with diamonds as trump

7♥ = Responder able to count at least seven tricks in
her own hand with hearts as trump

7♠ = Responder able to count at least seven tricks in
her own hand with spades as trump

7NT = 16-18 HCP.

Pass = 0-5 HCP, no five-card major

4♣ = Puppet Stayman

4♦ = Jacoby transfer to 4♥

4♥ = Jacoby transfer to 4♠

4♠ = MSS

4NT = 7-8 HCP, standard quantitative raise, invites to 6NT

5♣ = Void in clubs with 4♠-4♥-5♦-0♣ distribution; slam-going values

5♦ = Void in diamonds with 4♠-4♥-0♦-5♣ distribution; slam-going values

5♥ = Void in hearts with 4♠-0♥-5♦-4♣ or 4♠-0♥-4♦-5♣ distribution; slam-going values

5♠ = Void in spades with 0♠-4♥-5♦-4♣ or 0♠-4♥-4♦-5♣ distribution; slam-going values

5NT = Grand slam force; 12-13 HCP; opener should bid 6NT with a minimum or 7NT with a maximum

6♣ = 7-8 HCP, quantitative raise with help in clubs, invites to 6NT, but opener should feel confident to pass clubs

6♦ = 7-8 HCP, quantitative raise with help in diamonds, invites to 6NT, but opener should feel confident to pass diamonds

6♥ = 7-8 HCP, quantitative raise with help in hearts, invites to 6NT, but opener should feel confident to pass hearts

6♠ = 7-8 HCP, quantitative raise with help in spades, invites to 6NT, but opener should feel confident to pass spades

6NT = 9-10 HCP balanced, ends the auction.

7♣ = Responder able to count at least six tricks in her own hand with clubs as trump

7♦ = Responder able to count at least six tricks in her own hand with diamonds as trump

7♥ = Responder able to count at least six tricks in her own hand with hearts as trump

7♠ = Responder able to count at least six tricks in her own hand with spades as trump

7NT = 14-16 HCP.

The Gambling 3NT Opening

Opening 3NT to show a long running minor (i.e., no worse than AKQxxxx or AKJxxxxx), with no outside entry in first or second seat and no entry better than a guarded queen in third or fourth seat, no four-card major, and no voids, is known as the gambling 3NT. It is a very specific bid and its requirements must not be altered. Partner trusts you! With a void, a four-card major, or an outside entry, open 1 of the minor. With a long broken suit and no outside entry, preempt 3 or 4 of the minor.

If responder can readily infer which of the two minors opener intends to run, and if she has all three of the other suits stopped, then she can pass 3NT. Otherwise, she bids 4♣ as a run-out. If opener's suit is clubs, he passes. If it is diamonds, he corrects.

A gambling 3NT hand does not occur very often, but it occurs more often than a flat 25+ HCP hand, and thus the gambling 3NT is a useful bid. The enormous NT hand can always be described in other ways.

Forcing and Non-Forcing Stayman

Forcing Stayman, unlike the usual kind, does not promise a four-card major. Rather, it is a general-purpose force, by which responder, the captain, intends to elicit more information about opener's hand. Opener should treat responder's 2♦ forcing Stayman bid as if it asked for a four-card major, and rebid accordingly: 2♥ shows four hearts, 2♠ shows four spades, and 2NT shows neither four-card major. These are the only three rebids available to opener. With both four-card majors, she can rebid either, usually the better one. If responder rebids NT, she can then correct to the other major, if necessary, just as in plain old non-forcing Stayman.

After learning the information that opener's 2♥, 2♠, or 2NT rebid has conveyed, responder decides whether to bid game, sign off, invite to game, or explore for slam. Sign off below game is rare, and is generally done by passing opener's 2NT rebid when responder holds both four-card majors and the minimum in HCP. Responder's other possible rebids are similar to those with which we are all familiar from plain old Stayman.

Minor Suit Stayman

In using an artificial spade response to demand that opener choose between the two minors, we would like to be able to distinguish among responder's drop dead, game-invitational, game-forcing, and slam-exploratory intentions. We can usually do most of that. For game-force, it does not matter that the initial spade response is at a high level, say 4♠, but for the other three intentions, an initial response of 2♠ is usually wiser.

MSS absolutely promises five-five or better shape in the minors. In other words, responder's hand has the shape for an unusual NT overcall if the opponents had opened a major. Since responder guarantees five-five shape, openers in our system can rebid positively with only three cards in the chosen suit. Other versions of MSS specify that responder only needs to have five-four in the minors and no five-card major. In those versions, opener must have at least one four-card minor for a positive rebid. Our version works perfectly well because opener, by the definition of a NT opening, must have at least one three-card minor.

Opposite the 11½-14 HCP NT opening, we use 2♠ MSS strictly as a safety valve, part of our escape mechanism, allowing opener to run into a relatively safe contract in 3 of a minor, should the need arise. Thus for game-forcing or slam-exploratory MSS, 4♠ is the bid. For example:

```
Dealer: S        ♠ x
Vul.: Neither    ♥ x
                 ♦ A K Q x x x
                 ♣ A K J x x

♠ J x x x              N            ♠ Q x x x
♥ J x x x x       W    ♦    E       ♥ A x x x
♦ x x                  S            ♦ J x
♣ x x                               ♣ Q x x

                 ♠ A K x x
                 ♥ K Q x
                 ♦ x x x
                 ♣ x x x
```

South	West	North	East
1NT	pass	4♠	pass
5♣	pass	5♦	pass
pass	pass		

With longer and stronger diamonds, and knowing that opener has at least a doubleton, responder chooses to correct to diamonds rather than play in the known fit of at least eight cards in clubs. Either contract makes just five.

Since room for slam exploration is limited, it must be initiated by opener. Specifically, if opener has both four-card minors and is at the top of the HCP range, he bids 4NT. Responder then has a clear picture and knows exactly what to do:

```
Dealer: S          ♠ x
Vul.: Neither      ♥ x x
                   ♦ A K Q x x
                   ♣ A K J x x

♠ x x x x x               ♠ Q J x x x
♥ x x x x x x    N        ♥ A J
♦ —          W  ✧  E      ♦ J x x x
♣ x x            S        ♣ x x

                   ♠ A K
                   ♥ K Q x
                   ♦ x x x x
                   ♣ Q x x x
```

South	West	North	East
1NT	pass	4♣	pass
4NT	pass	6♦	pass
pass	pass		

North, the captain, chooses the slam rather than game and 6♦ rather than 6♣ because the suit is stronger. If the lengths were unequal, he would choose the longer, regardless of strength. He is not worried about his small doubleton, because he infers from partner's 4NT that she has honors in the majors and at least one ace.

The slam goes down one, but not because of bad bidding. Most Standard American pairs would be in 6 of a minor as well. The results across the field should provide close to a flat board. There is just no way to predict four-zero trump splits in uncontested auctions.

Checkback Stayman

In standard bidding, if you open a minor, partner responds 1♥, and you rebid 1♠, then partner knows that you have exactly four spades, but does not know anything (yet) about your hearts. Moreover, and most importantly, you have not yet limited your hand.

Also, in standard bidding, if you open a minor, partner responds 1♥, and you rebid 1NT, then you deny having as many as four spades.

In AWNT, if you open a minor, partner responds 1♥, and you rebid 1♠, you show exactly four spades, but deny NT shape. You might have something like ♠Qxxx ♥x ♦AJxx ♣KQxx or ♠AQxx ♥— ♦AJxx ♣KQxxx. Your rebid is unlimited.

Also in AWNT, if you open a minor, partner responds 1♥, and you rebid 1NT, you promise 15-17 HCP, but you do not deny having as many as three hearts or four spades. Partner can then find out more about your holdings in the majors by rebidding an artificial 2♣ as "checkback Stayman" (CBS).[3]

Checkback is always available, regardlesss of the NT range, after a minor suit opening and a major suit response. The basic sequence is 1♣/♦ - 1♥/♠ -1NT - 2♣. Opener's bid is a convenient minor. Responder's bid shows at least four in that major and implies the usual Standard American set of possible relationships to the other major. Opener's rebid shows 15-17 HCP flat, denying four-card support, but not denying either three cards in responder's major or four in the other major. If opener had four in responder's major, she would rebid 2 of that major, as described above in Chapter 2. Responder's rebid of 2♣ is completely artificial, asking opener to show either three cards in his major or four in the other major. Opener's first duty then becomes to support the original major, if possible, and her second duty to show the other major, again if possible.

In traditional CBS, opener's 2♦ rebid shows a

---

[3] Not to be confused with either the Columbia Broadcasting System or "checkbook Stayman," in which we pay our partner to have four cards in our major.

hand with neither three in responder's major nor four in the other major, while the 2NT rebid shows both three in responder's and four in the other. This system of rebids has two main disadvantages: (1) The denial of both suits leaves responder not knowing what to do at the 2-level and renders problematic whether her 2NT rebid would be drop dead or invitational; and (2) the affirmation of both suits forces the pair to the 3-level.

Thus we prefer reverse checkback (reverse CBS or RCBS), in which the meanings of these two rebids are flip-flopped, i.e., 2♦ shows both three in responder's major and four in the other, while 2NT shows neither three in responder's nor four in the other. This system has two main advantages: (1) Responder can pass 2NT if he does not like the news; and (2) he can rebid 2 of his preferred major as a drop dead bid or 3 of his major as invitational.

So, with 2♦ = "both" and 2NT = "neither," the full schedule of opener's rebids is:

2♦ = Both three-card support and four cards in the other major

2♥ when responder has bid 1♥ = Exactly three hearts and either two or three spades

2♥ when responder has bid 1♠ = Exactly four hearts and exactly two spades

2♠ when responder has bid 1♥ = Exactly four spades and exactly two hearts

2♠ when responder has bid 1♠ = Exactly three spades and either two or three hearts

2NT = Neither three-card support nor four cards in the other major

Most K-S and all AWNT openers bypass a four-card spade suit in order to rebid 1NT to show 15-17 HCP after responder has bid 1♥. Then the "both" response to checkback (either 2♦ or 2NT, by partnership agreement) shows exactly three hearts and four spades.

Other K-S openers (including Edgar Kaplan himself) rebid 1♠ in this situation, thus leaving opener's HCP count ambiguous through the second round. Then the 2NT response to CBS does not exist, since opener must now use it to show 15-17 HCP. By rebidding 2♣, responder denies having as many as four spades, and shows exactly five hearts. While it is indeed for each partnership to agree which of these two methods to use, I must say that I find Kaplan's original method bizarre and counterproductive. It is not nearly as versatile and cannot handle the most common situations as efficiently.

Here is an example of using reverse CBS to find a double fit in the majors:

Dealer: S   ♠ x x x x
Vul.: Both   ♥ A K x x x
                     ♦ x
                     ♣ x x x

♠ A Q J   ♠ x x
♥ x x   N   ♥ J x x
♦ x x x x x   W   ✧   E   ♦ K Q J x
♣ x x x   S   ♣ Q J x x

                     ♠ K x x x
                     ♥ Q x x
                     ♦ A x x
                     ♣ A K x

South	West	North	East
1♦	pass	1♥	pass
1NT	pass	2♣	pass
2♦	pass	3♠	pass
4♠	pass	pass	pass

After opener's artificial 2♦, responder could bid 2 of either major as a drop dead signal, bid 3 to invite, or leap directly to game. With this hand, the invitation seems best. Opener accepts and the 23 HCP game makes.

Puppet Stayman

The purpose of puppet Stayman is to enable opener, whose hand includes a five-card major, to bid NT without misleading partner. The ranges of NT openings for which puppet Stayman is in effect are fixed by partnership agreement. I prefer to play it only for the higher ranges, leaving the lower ranges — at which there are so many other ways for opener to show a five-card major — rigorously free of the possibility of five-card majors hidden in hands that are opened in NT.

Among the advantages of puppet Stayman is that a description of the probable dummy's hand rather than (as in other forms of Stayman) a description of the probable declarer's hand is what is revealed to the opponents. Its two main disadvantages are that (1) it cannot be played effectively unless in conjunction with Jacoby transfers and (2) responder's rebids are very complicated after 1NT and so compressed after 2NT that showing certain kinds of common hands becomes difficult. The reason why Jacoby transfers must be used is that responder, in order to bid puppet Stayman, may not hold a five-card major with three or fewer in the other major. There is no room in the puppet Stayman system to describe this hand. But Jacoby can handle it.

The basic idea of puppet Stayman is that — using a 1-level weak or strong NT opening as an example — responder's 2♣ is a qualified relay to 2♦. Opener must rebid 2♦ unless holding a five-card major, which she must then bid directly, or unless holding no four-card major, in which case she must rebid 2NT. Responder's rebids after opener's 2♦ promises at least one four-card major then are:

2♥ = Four spades, no more than three hearts, invitational values, relay to spades or NT

2♠ = Four hearts, no more than three spades, invitational values, relay to hearts or NT

2NT = Both four-card majors, invitational values

3♣ = Five hearts, four spades, invitational values, relay to hearts, spades, or NT

3♦ = Five spades, four hearts, invitational values, relay to hearts, spades, or NT

3♥ = Four spades, no more than three hearts, game-forcing values, relay to spades or NT

3♠ = Four hearts, no more than three spades, game-forcing values, relay to hearts or NT

3NT = Both four-card majors, game-forcing values

4♣ = Five hearts, four spades, game-forcing values, relay to hearts or spades

4♦ = Five spades, four hearts, game-forcing values, relay to hearts or spades

Responder's rebids after opener's 2♥ rebid shows a five-card heart suit are:

2♠ = Three hearts and four spades, invitational values, relay to hearts or NT

2NT = Four spades and no more than two hearts, invitational values

3♣ = Four hearts and four spades, invitational values, relay to hearts or NT

3♦ = Three hearts and four spades, game-forcing values, relay to hearts or NT

3♥ = Four hearts and four spades, game-forcing values, relay to hearts or NT

3♠ = Four hearts and no more than three spades, relay to hearts or NT

3NT = Four spades and no more than two hearts, game-forcing values

4♣ = Five spades and four hearts, relay to hearts

4♦ = Five hearts and four spades, relay to hearts

Responder's rebids after opener's 2♠ rebid shows a five-card spade suit are:

2NT = Four hearts and no more than two spades, invitational values

3♣ = Four hearts and three spades, invitational values, relay to spades or NT

3♦ = Four hearts and four spades, invitational values, relay to spades or NT

3♥ = Four hearts and three spades, game-forcing values, relay to spades or NT

3♠ = Four hearts and four spades, game-forcing values, relay to spades or NT

3NT = Four hearts and no more than two spades, game-forcing values

4♣ = Five hearts and four spades, relay to spades

4♦ = Five spades and four hearts, relay to spades

4♥ = Four spades and no more than three hearts, relay to spades

Responder's rebids after opener's 2NT rebid shows no longer than a three-card major are:

3♣ = Five spades and four hearts, drop dead values, relay to spades

3♦ = Five hearts and four spades, drop dead values, relay to hearts

3♥ = Five spades and four hearts, invitational values, relay to spades or NT

3♠ = Five hearts and four spades, invitational values, relay to hearts or NT

3NT = No more than four hearts and no more than four spades; opener should pass

4♣ = Gerber

4♦ = Five hearts and four spades, game-forcing values, relay to hearts

4♥ = Five spades and four hearts, game-forcing values, relay to spades

A few modifications are needed for using puppet Stayman with 2-level NT openings or sequences. After responder's artificial 3♣, opener's rebids are:

3♦ = Undisclosed four-card major(s), no five-card major
3♥ = Five-card heart suit
3♠ = Five-card spade suit
3NT = No four-card major

Responder's rebids after opener's 3♦ shows at least one four-card major are:

3♥ = Four spades, three or fewer hearts, relay to
   either spades or NT
3♠ = Four hearts, three or fewer spades, relay to
   either hearts or NT
3NT = Four cards in each major; opener may either
   pass or correct to either hearts or spades
4♣ = Five hearts and four spades, relay to either
   hearts or spades
4♦ = Five spades and four hearts, relay to either
   hearts or spades

Responder's rebids after opener's 3♥ rebid shows a five-card heart suit are:

3♠ = Four hearts, any number of spades, relay to
   hearts
3NT = Four spades, no more than two hearts; opener
   should usually pass
4♣ = Three hearts and four spades, relay to hearts
4♦ = Five hearts and four spades, relay to hearts

Responder's rebids after opener's 3♠ rebid shows a five-card spade suit are:

3NT = Four hearts, no more than two spades; opener
   should usually pass
4♣ = Four spades, any number of hearts, relay to
   spades
4♦ = Three spades and four hearts, relay to spades
4♥ = Five spades and four hearts, relay to spades

Responder's rebids are non-existent after opener's 3NT rebid shows no major longer than three-cards, unless responder possesses slam exploratory values. If he does not pass opener's 3NT, he may either bid 4NT as Blackwood or start bidding suits — even clubs — up the line on the 4-level as control-showing cue bids.

Jacoby and Texas Transfers

The purpose of Jacoby and Texas transfers is to keep the stronger hand concealed as declarer. Artificially bid the suit under the intended suit at the 2-level for Jacoby or the suit under the intended suit at the 4-level for Texas.

At the appropriate levels of the NT opening — and this can be decided by partnership agreement — opener can superaccept the Jacoby transfer. That means that opener jump accepts to show four pieces of trump and the top end of the HCP range. Superacceptance is an excellent way to convey extra information to the captain of the auction. As opener, you have already limited your hand to a narrow HCP range by bidding NT, but now you have the opportunity to limit it even further, not only eliminating the lower end of the HCP range, but also telling partner something about your shape.

Jacoby transfers are off in competition, and the bid that would have been the artificial transfer relay becomes natural and — usually — drop dead.

Texas transfers are always on, through an overcall of 4♣ if responder's suit is hearts and through an overcall of 4♦ if responder's suit is spades. Since opener could have as few as two in the suit, but must have at least that many, responder promises at least six in the suit to ensure an eight-card fit at the 4-level.

When is 4♣ Gerber?

Edith McMullin tells an interesting story about how a certain bridge player would not take the word of even John Gerber himself for when a 4♣ bid is the Gerber ace-asking convention.[4] The story is not only hilarious, but also illustrates a genuine and persistent problem: recognizing Gerber.

It is indeed a plain fact that Gerber is difficult to recognize. I confess that there was a time in my bridge playing career when I refused to play Gerber at all, because it was so confusing. I gave up the quantitative NT raise and treated all 4NT responses as Blackwood. No great loss, actually.

Nowadays I have outgrown this reticence and am willing to play Gerber. But I add it to my convention card only after my partner and I have agreed in detailed and explicit terms when 4♣ is and is not Gerber.

First of all, Gerber is always a jump bid. The 3NT - 4♣ sequence can never be Gerber.

Second, Gerber occurs only when the established strain is NT. This establishment can take only seven forms: the 1NT opening, the 1♣/♦ - 1NT sequence, the 1♣/♦ - 2NT sequence, the 2NT opening, the 2♣ - 2♦/♥/♠ - 2NT sequence, the strong NT direct-seat overcall of the opponents' opening suit bid, and the direct-seat penalty double of the opponents' opening 1NT.[5]

Finally, Gerber is off if opener is overcalled and is generally off in competition. Yet it is on if the other side has opened and our side, in direct seat, has either

---

[4] Edith Titterton McMullin, *Adventures in Duplicate Bridge* (Memphis: ACBL, 1989), p. 38.

[5] See the full discussions of these competitive sequences below in the "No Trump Overcalls" section of this chapter and in Chapter 11 on defensive bidding, pp. 152-153.

overcalled their suit with a strong NT or doubled their opening 1NT for penalty.

After an opening NT or NT-showing sequence at any level, the 4NT response is quantitative if and only if Gerber is available. Otherwise, it is Blackwood.

There is a beautiful, altogether remarkable, but underappreciated aspect of Gerber. Say your partner opens 1NT, either weak or strong, or a strong 2NT, and you have a shapely but weakish hand that re-evaluates to game-going but not slam-going values opposite partner's hand. You also have two or fewer aces, no worse than five-five shape in the majors, and tolerance for a final contract of 4NT if partner has three aces. Bid 4♣. Partner will assume it is Gerber, asking for aces, but you know — as partner will also soon find out — that it is really a takeout bid for the majors. If partner bids either 4♥, showing one ace, or 4♠, showing two aces, you pass. If partner bids 4♦, showing no aces or all the aces, you rebid 4♥, showing your major suit shape and your non-Gerber intentions. Partner now knows what's what, and will either pass 4♥ with three or more hearts or correct to 4♠ if that seems better.

ConFit

Among the most powerful weapons in our slam bidding arsenal is ConFit. The name of this convention refers to "*Controls*" and "*Fit*," that is, the two components of a successful slam which it seeks to discover.

Sometimes when a side has a combined HCP total of less than the 33 or 34 usually required for a small slam, it can still take twelve tricks in a suit contract if it has an eight-card fit and sufficient first and second-round controls. This may be true even if the side has two flat hands totalling only about 30 HCP. Yet too many of these borderline slams remain unbid. The purpose of ConFit is to make them biddable. Many hands play in 3NT making five that could just as well play in six of a suit making six; and many hands play in four of a major making six that could just as well play in six making six. Indeed 920s, 980s, 1370s, and 1430s look much better on a scorecard than 420s, 480s, 620s, and 680s. The skillful use of ConFit can make this big difference, equally at IMPs and matchpoints, with very little risk.

The "Controls" account for 28 of the 40 HCP in the deck, namely, all the aces and kings. An ace is two controls, a king is one. There are twelve controls in the deck. A side can generally make a small slam if it has ten controls, i.e., if it is missing no more than either an ace or two kings. A standard 15-17 HCP 1NT opening hand could have a minimum of one control (four queens, four jacks, and a king) or a maximum of eight (four aces). An 11½-14 HCP 1NT opening hand could have no controls at all or a maximum of six (either three aces or two aces and two kings). A strong 20-21 HCP 2NT opening hand has at least three controls (four queens, three jacks, and three kings) but can have a maximum of nine (four aces and one king).

The "Fit" is defined as four-four, no worse than Kxxx-Qxxx. Accordingly, no suit may be mentioned naturally by either opener or responder in a ConFit auction unless it is at least as good as Qxxx. The one exception is that, if opener shows a five-card suit, responder may support it with as little as Qxx.

The basic idea of ConFit is this: If responder has a flat hand (no five-card suit, no singleton or void, and no more than one doubleton), sufficient HCP to believe that the side is in the vicinity of 30-33 total, sufficient controls to suspect that the side may have the ten controls normally needed for slam, and at least one four-card suit no worse than Qxxx, then responder may initiate a ConFit inquiry by bidding the cheapest number of spades. Responder thus becomes the captain of the auction. Opener then rebids in artificial steps showing controls. If not satisfied with opener's controls, responder may immediately shut off the auction by bidding the cheapest NT.

Whenever responder bids any level of no trump, the auction is over. Opener must pass. If, however, opener's controls are to responder's liking, responder may continue the slam exploration by starting to bid four-card suits up the line until a fit is found. The fit is announced by either bidder raising the other's bid. A jump raise shows either a four-card suit with two of the top three honors or a five-card suit no worse than Qxxxx; otherwise a single raise is used. (Recall that only opener's hand may contain a five-card suit.) During the search for a fit, opener shows a five-carder by jumping into it at the very first opportunity, either as a raise or as a new suit. Responder may support opener's five-card suit with only three pieces, but no worse than Qxx.

Opposite a weak NT opening, responder should have between a good 16 and a bad 19 HCP; opposite a 15-17 HCP NT opening, between a good 13 and a bad 16 HCP; and opposite a 2NT opening, between a good 9 and a bad 13. That is, the total of the two hands should be between about 30 and 33 HCP.

Six steps are defined to show controls after the 2♠ or 3♠ relay, laid out according to the strength of the opening:

11½-14 HCP:	15-17 HCP:	20-21 HCP:
2NT = 0-1	2NT = 1-3	3NT = 3-4
3♣ = 2	3♣ = 4	4♣ = 5
3♦ = 3	3♦ = 5	4♦ = 6
3♥ = 4	3♥ = 6	4♥ = 7
3♠ = 5	3♠ = 7	4♠ = 8
3NT = 6	3NT = 8	4NT = 9

A typical weak NT ConFit auction may proceed like this:

<u>Opener:</u> 1NT = "I have 11½-14 HCP flat and maybe a five-card minor."

<u>Responder:</u> 2♠ = "I have between a good 16 and a bad 19 HCP, a flat hand, no five-card suit, and am interested in slam. I am not strong enough either to make a quantitative raise or to insist on slam. How many controls do you have?"

<u>Op.:</u> 3♥ = "I have four controls."

<u>Resp.:</u> 3♠ = "OK, we have at least ten controls. Let's try to find a fit. I have four spades."

<u>Op.:</u> 4♦ = "I don't have either four spades or four clubs or a five-card suit, but I have four diamonds."

<u>Resp.:</u> 4♥ = "I don't have four diamonds, but I have four hearts."

<u>Op.:</u> 4NT = "I don't have any other four-card suits."

<u>Resp.:</u> Pass = "OK, let's shut it off here. We have the controls but not the fit, so I guess we can't make slam."

Responder, in this case, may pass 4NT confident that the side has not missed a biddable slam. That is, even if opener should turn out to be at the top of the range with 14 HCP, responder knows that (1) the combined HCP total is not strong enough to make 6NT, and (2) slam is almost surely out of reach without an eight-card fit.

In our system, since we use 2♠ as MSS, we play ConFit only after either an opening 2NT or an opening 2♣ with a NT rebid. So, one of our typical ConFit auctions may proceed like this:

<u>Op.:</u> 2NT = "1 have 20-21 HCP, flat, and maybe a five-card suit, even a major."

<u>Resp.:</u> 2♠ = "I have between a good 9 and a bad 12 HCP, a flat hand, no five-card suit, and am in-

terested in slam. I am not strong enough either to make a quantitative raise or to insist on slam. How many controls do you have?"

Op.: 3♥ = "I have seven controls."

Resp.: 4♣ = "OK, we have at least ten controls. Let's try to find a fit. I don't have four spades, but I have four clubs."

Op.: 5♦ = "I don't have four spades, but I have five diamonds."

Resp.: 5NT = "I don't have three diamonds or any other four-card suits, so I'm shutting the auction off now. I am ordering you to pass."

Op.: Pass = "Aye, aye, Captain!"

Another of our typical ConFit auctions — with a happier ending — may look like this:

Op.: 2NT = "1 have 20-21 HCP, flat, and maybe a five-card suit, even a major."

Resp.: 2♠ = "I have between a good 9 and a bad 12 HCP, a flat hand, no five-card suit, and am interested in slam. I am not strong enough either to make a quantitative raise or to insist on slam. How many controls do you have?"

Op.: 3♥ = "I have seven controls."

Resp.: 3♠ = "OK, we have at least ten controls. Let's try to find a fit. I have four spades."

Op.: 4♣ = "I don't have either four spades or a five-card suit, but I have four clubs."

Resp.: 4♦ = "I don't have four clubs, but I have four diamonds."

Op.: 5♦ = "So do I. Great! There's our four-four fit!"

Resp.: 6♦ = "Excellent! Let's do the slam."

Op.: Pass = "Go get 'em, Tiger!"

The ranges of ConFit control-asking and control-showing bids can easily be adjusted for other ranges of NT. The 22-23 HCP NT hand has between four (all the jacks, three queens, and all the kings) and ten (all four

aces and two kings) controls. The 24-25 hand has between four (all the jacks, queens, and kings) and eleven
(all four aces and three kings) controls.

Showing a No Trump
Hand in Competition

When opener has a 15-17 or 18-19 HCP flat hand, she
can sometimes show a stopper in an enemy suit with
her rebid in the second round. There are four typical
cases:

In the first situation, she opens her convenient
minor. LHO passes. Partner passes, showing 0-5 HCP.
RHO bids a suit on the 1-level. She can then pass to
show 15-17 HCP without a stopper, bid 1NT to show
15-17 HCP with a stopper, cue bid the enemy suit to
show 18-19 HCP without a stopper, bid 2NT to show
18-19 HCP with a stopper, or double as a strong three-
suited takeout.

Similarly, after she opens her convenient minor,
LHO bids a suit on the 1-level. Responder and RHO
both pass. She can then reopen with a double to show
15-17 HCP without a stopper, bid 1NT to show 15-17
HCP with a stopper, cue bid the enemy suit to show
18-19 HCP without a stopper, or bid 2NT to show 18-
19 HCP with a stopper.

Again, when RHO balances at the 2-level, opener's
pass shows inability or unwillingness to compete with
15-17 HCP opposite responder's weak hand. Her double shows 15 or more HCP with a strong stopper and is
penalty oriented. Her cue bid shows 18-19 HCP without a stopper and her bid of 2NT shows 18-19 HCP
with a stopper.

Finally, when LHO overcalls on the 2-level, opener's pass shows that she expects the opponents' contract to fail. Her reopening double is a three-suited takeout, demanding that responder run out to the cheapest playable suit. Her cue bid shows 18-19 HCP without a stopper and her bid of 2NT shows 18-19 HCP with a stopper.

Her pass or double is forcing in all cases. Her cue bid is "Western-ish," asking for, but not really expecting, given responder's already announced weakness, a stopper in the enemy suit. Her NT rebids are forcing to a run-out suit when responder is at the lower end of the HCP range for his pass, but not forcing when responder is at the high end of that range and can tolerate being dummy at that level of NT.

No Trump Overcalls

Overcalling the opening side is generally a defensive or obstructive bidding maneuver. But when you overcall the opening 1-level suit bid with 1NT, showing 15-18 HCP and a stopper in the opening suit, you are really going on the offensive, attempting to seize the initiative from the opening side. In direct seat you have an even bigger advantage, since your 15-18 are behind opener's 11+ HCP. Because the strong 1NT overcall is an offensive rather than a defensive bid, we discuss it here instead of below in Chapter 10 on overcalls or in Chapter 11 on defensive bidding.

As soon as the 1NT overcall is made, everyone at the table knows where at least 26 of the 40 HCP are. Responder and advancer can each look at their own hands, do the simple math, and infer what the other probably has. The odds strongly favor that the 1NT overcalling side owns the deal. If advancer has 6 or a good 5 HCP, that ownership is assured, and he should quickly apprise overcaller of this fact, if possible.

In order to facilitate communication between overcaller and advancer, we play that the full schedule of strong NT systems are on opposite the 1NT overcall, just as if the 1NT bid had been a Standard American 15-17 HCP NT opening.[6] So:

> 2♣ = Plain old Stayman
> 2♦ = Jacoby transfer to 2♥ (or to 3♥ with super-
>   acceptance)
> 2♥ = Jacoby transfer to 2♠ (or to 3♠ with super-
>   acceptance)
> 2♠ = MSS
> 2NT = Invitation to 3NT
> 3♣ = Drop dead, to play in clubs
> 3♦ = Drop dead, to play in diamonds
> 3♥ = Forcing to game in either hearts or NT
> 3♠ = Forcing to game in either spades or NT
> 3NT = To play
> 4♣ = Gerber
> 4♦ = Texas transfer to 4♥
> 4♥ = Texas transfer to 4♠

In the balance seat, i.e., after LHO's 1-level suit bid and two passes, we also follow Standard American practice to agree that 1NT shows 11-14 HCP, a stopper, and no biddable suit. With this hand but no stopper, the balancer would reopen with a double.

---

[6] We also play that the same system is on opposite a penalty double of the opponents' 1NT opening. See Chapter 11, pp. 152-153.

5

Escapes

If you are going to play the weak NT, you will need to have a sophisticated, versatile, and comprehensive system of escapes. That is, if you are going to open so many more hands 1NT than you would if you were playing the 15-17 or 16-18 HCP range, you are going to find yourself in more situations that you cannot handle at 1NT. You must then have convenient means to drop the contract at 2 — or even 3 or more — of a suit, which almost always plays better than 1NT when declarer and dummy together own fewer than 20 HCP.

Opposite a strong NT opening, partner needs only about 3 or 4 HCP for the hand to be playable at 1NT. But this measure of safety cannot be assured opposite a weak NT opening unless partner has at least 7 or 8 HCP. Obviously partner has at least 7 HCP less often than she has at least 3.

After Doubles

Opponents are not reluctant to double weak 1NT openings for penalty — especially in the direct seat. Some

pairs will do it with as few as 12 or 13 HCP, although
most will have the expected 15-18. When this double
happens the so-called "run-out sequence" (ROS) is on
for the opening side, and the responder who holds 8 or
fewer HCP is faced with just a few choices, determined
only by the shape of that hand.

First, consider the situation when responder has
at least one five-card suit. Unless responder is a passed
hand, we do not play Jacoby transfers with the weak
1NT opening, for reasons discussed above in Chapter
4, and they would be off in competition anyway. But
over a direct-seat double, Jacoby transfers (or something similar) are "on" — in a sense. That is, we use a
system of transfer escapes (sometimes known as "Moscow escapes") to drop the contract in a suit at the 2-
level with the 1NT opener as declarer. When 1NT is
doubled in direct seat, and when responder has 0-6 (or
a bad 7) HCP and any suit of at least five cards, the
transfer escape responses are:

> Redouble = transfer to clubs
> 2♣ = transfer to diamonds
> 2♦ = transfer to hearts
> 2♥ = transfer to spades

Note that 2♠, an otherwise idle bid, can be used in this
situation as a drop dead at the 3-level version of MSS,
a takeout for the minors, showing a weak hand with
five-five or better shape in those suits.

Responder *could* use a 2-level transfer escape
with a *really* bad hand and a six or even a seven-card
suit; but with weak-to-moderate playing strength in
responder's hand and a six-card or longer major, a
Texas transfer is usually preferable in the 1NT doubled
situation, if only for its preemptive value. Even if
opener has the full 14 HCP while responder has a yarborough with a six-card suit, the Texas-style escape,
guaranteeing an eight-card fit, is practically *de rigueur*,

since it creates difficulties for the opponents trying to figure out how to use their 26 HCP to their best advantage. The final level of play must be determined in the first round by responder (the captain) according to the Principle of Fast Arrival. Opener cannot do it because he does not have enough information. If responder makes a 2-level transfer, opener will naturally expect her to have only five cards in that suit.

Escaping from a direct-seat double of an 11½-14 1NT opening is just that easy when responder has a five-card suit and a bad hand. But the case is more complicated — and more dangerous — when responder has the same bad hand but no suit longer than four. This is when responder must bring the ROS into the auction. It works as follows:

After RHO's direct double of partner's opening weak 1NT, your pass absolutely 100% denies that you hold a five-card or longer suit and absolutely 100% demands that partner redouble if LHO passes. It says nothing — yet — about your HCP count. This pass is alertable because it functions as a relay. If LHO asks partner to explain your pass, all he has to say is something like, "It's a forcing pass, denying a five-card suit. It might be the beginning of our run-out sequence. I'm required to redouble if you pass."

Of course, if LHO bids after your forcing pass, you and partner can both breathe easy. You have escaped! The opponents have cut your ROS short and have made it unnecessary. You and partner are now both free to pass without fear, if you wish, for the rest of the auction.

But, if LHO passes and partner duly redoubles, then, with 0 to about a bad 9 HCP, bid your cheapest four-card suit. You and partner will now bid four-card suits up the line until either you find a tolerable fit at the 2-level or the opponents bail you out by overcalling. That is the whole ROS.

But, after your initial forcing pass, you as responder have many other options available besides the ROS. Their full schedule is:

Pass. With about a good 9 to a middling 11 HCP and adequate controls behind doubler, pass the redouble. This promises partner that you believe he can make 1NT redoubled, even if he has a minimum. Passing your partner's redouble puts enormous pressure on the opponents. Making 1NT redoubled is game! Now they are the ones who must run! You and partner may now chuckle quietly but ethically to yourselves.

2NT. Your 2NT response after RHO's double is natural, showing a balanced 12-13 HCP with invitational qualities, good controls behind doubler, and probably no five-card suit. Partner should bid 3NT with a maximum or pass with a minimum.

3♣/♦/♥/♠. Even over RHO's double, your bid of 3 of any suit is forcing to game, usually in either 3NT or a major. It guarantees at least a seven-card suit or an exceptional six-card suit, tends to show an extremely distributional hand with good controls, and suggests slam interest. With minimal support for your suit, partner should sign off at 3NT. With good support, he can sign off in your suit. With excellent support and a maximum HCP count, he can begin slam exploration by either bidding Blackwood or cue bidding a new suit to show a first-round control.

3NT. Sign off with 14+ HCP balanced, good controls behind doubler, and probably no five-card suit. At this point your LHO is marked with a lousy hand, probably no more than 2 or 3 HCP when partner and your RHO each have minimums.

4♣. Gerber.

4♦. Texas transfer to hearts, guaranteeing at least a six-card suit.

4♥. Texas transfer to spades, guaranteeing at least a six-card suit.

4♠. Unlike the 2♠ response above, this is a very strong

MSS. Rather than a drop dead take-out for the minors, five-five or better, it shows a highly distributional hand with excellent controls that can tolerate game in a minor opposite any holding opener may have. Mainly it shows slam interest, so opener should rebid 6 of his better minor directly with maximum HCP, 5 of his better minor directly with minimum HCP, 5NT with maximum HCP and equal length in the minors, or 4NT with minimum HCP and equal length in the minors. After opener's NT rebid, responder will then choose the minor to play at the cheapest level.

With an MSS-shaped hand and sufficient strength to explore for slam, it might sometimes be better to start the exploration with 4♣ Gerber instead of 4♠ MSS, especially when the suits are of unequal length. Generally speaking — but responder really must rely on intuition here — bid Gerber when the two minors are of comparable strength but unequal length; but bid MSS with possibly weaker and shapelier hands and either equal length in the minors or unequal length when the longer minor is significantly weaker than the shorter. This deal, for example, bids more accurately with Gerber:

```
Dealer: N          ♠ Q x x
Vul.: Neither      ♥ A x x
                   ♦ A J x
                   ♣ J x x x

♠ x x x x x              N        ♠ K J x x
♥ x x x x x        W    ◇    E    ♥ K Q J x
♦ x x                   S        ♦ x x
♣ x                              ♣ A x x

                   ♠ A
                   ♥ x
                   ♦ K Q x x x x
                   ♣ K Q x x x
```

North	East	South	West
1NT	Double	4♣	Pass
4♠	Pass	6♦	Pass
Pass	Pass		

Even with only 14 HCP, South knows that twelve tricks are almost assured if North has any two aces. If North had answered either 4♦ (no aces) or 4♥ (one ace), South could easily shut the auction off at 4NT. Trade North's two aces for two kings and two jacks from East, and 4NT should make easily:

Dealer: N   ♠ K Q J
Vul.: Neither   ♥ K J x
               ♦ J x x
               ♣ J x x x

♠ x x x x x   ♠ x x x x
♥ x x x x x   N   ♥ A Q x x
♦ x x   W ✧ E   ♦ A x
♣ x   S   ♣ A x x

            ♠ A
            ♥ x
            ♦ K Q x x x x
            ♣ K Q x x x

With a triple stopper in spades and a double stopper in hearts, declarer has plenty of time to set up the minors.

But with a hand such as ♠A ♥A ♦xxxxxx ♣AQxxx or ♠A ♥— ♦xxxxxxx ♣AKQxx, the deal would bid more elegantly if responder began with 4♠ MSS. In any event, Gerber and Blackwood are impossible if the inquirer has a void.

That takes care of all the possibilities when our weak 1NT opening is doubled in direct seat. But what about when this 1NT is passed twice then doubled in the balance seat? Our system of escapes from the balancing double of the weak 1NT[1] is a lot more complex than either the basic "Pass → Redouble" ROS or the 2-level transfer escape system, but it is every bit as necessary to ensure safety.

First of all, let us analyze, from opener's point of view, what those two passes before the balancing double might show: "LHO might be trap passing or might be just too weak to double or too short to bid. Partner might be able to tolerate 1NT, or she might be unable to tolerate it yet still have a hand that does not allow either garbage Stayman or a drop dead bid in a long suit. Yet partner might have a five-card suit, and if so, it is likely a minor, since she could have dropped dead at the 2-level with a major. Indeed, her 0-6 HCP flat hand would be a worst case scenario. If partner's hand has no five-card suit, it must be 0-10 HCP, because, if she had 11+, she would have invited with 2NT or bid 3NT outright. RHO could have as few as 8 HCP for his reopening double, or he could have a monster."

So, in that situation, the opponents together have at least 16 HCP, since opener's maximum is 14 and responder's is 10. More likely, the HCP are closer to evenly divided between the two pairs. This is a very dangerous predicament for the opening side!

There are only two basic shapes that opener's NT hand could have: Either he has a five-card minor or he has no five-card suit. Now you might think that if opener has a five-card minor, he should just bid it directly after the balancing double. But there are two excellent reasons not to do this:

First, this case is not analogous to that in which responder, after the direct-seat double, transfers opener into her five-card suit. She knows that opener has at

---

[1] Credit for inventing this system of escapes belongs to Cameron Ross. I call them "Baldwinsville Escapes" after the village where he lives. I admit to having added a few features that he might neither recognize nor agree with.

least a doubleton in that suit and she knows opener's HCP range within 3 points. But, for all opener knows, the passed responder might have a yarborough and a void in opener's five-card minor.

Second, again, for all opener knows, responder might have 9-10 HCP with good controls. 1NT might make. Responder might want to convert that balancing double to penalty.

For these two reasons, another mechanism must be found for opener to tell responder that he has a five-card minor.

We therefore agree that, after the balancing double, only two calls are available to the 1NT opener: (1) redouble to show that the hand contains a five-card suit, which must be a minor, and (2) pass to show that the hand contains no five-card suit. Responder has many options after opener either passes or redoubles the opponents' balancing double.

When opener redoubles, thus showing a five-card minor but not specifying the NT range any narrower than 11½-14 HCP, responder's possible calls are:

Pass. Converts the redouble to penalty.

2♣. Artificial; shows a weak hand and the desire to play in opener's five-card minor. Opener will pass if his suit is clubs or correct to 2♦ if it is diamonds.

2♦. Shows exactly four diamonds; denies any five-card suit; says nothing about club length; starts sequence of bidding four-card suits up the line until at least a four-three fit is found.

2♥. Shows exactly four hearts; denies any five-card suit and as many as four diamonds; says nothing about club length; starts sequence of bidding four-card suits up the line until at least a four-three fit is found.

2♠. Shows exactly four spades; denies any five-card suit and as many as four diamonds or four hearts; says nothing about club length; starts sequence of bidding four-card suits up the line until at least a four-three fit is found.

2NT. Artificially shows exactly four clubs; denies any five-card suit and as many as four cards in any of the other three suits, thereby revealing shape as exactly 3♠-3♥-3♦-4♣; starts sequence of bidding four-card suits up the line until at least a four-three fit is found.

3♣. Drop dead; shows five clubs.

3♦. Drop dead; shows five diamonds.

3♥. Drop dead; shows five hearts; but probably responder should already, at her first chance to respond, have dropped dead at the 2-level.

3♠. Drop dead; shows five spades; but again, probably responder should already have dropped dead.

When opener passes, thus denying any suit longer than four but perhaps having as many as two four-card suits, responder's calls are:

Pass. Converts the double to penalty.

Redouble. Transfer to 2♣; promises a five-card suit — not necessarily clubs — and shows a weak hand that would play better in a five-two fit at the 2-level than in NT. After opener completes the transfer, responder will, if necessary, correct to 2 of her actual five-card suit.

2♣. Shows exactly four clubs; denies any five-card suit; starts sequence of bidding four-card suits up the line until at least a four-three fit is found.

2♦. Shows exactly four diamonds; denies any five-card suit and as many as four clubs; starts sequence of bidding four-card suits up the line until at least a four-three fit is found.

2♥. Shows exactly four hearts; denies any five-card suit and as many as four clubs or four diamonds; starts sequence of bidding four-card suits up the line until at least a four-three fit is found.

2♠. Shows exactly four spades; denies any five-card suit and as many as four in any of the other three suits, thereby revealing shape as exactly 4♠-3♥-3♦-3♣; starts sequence of bidding four-card suits up the line until at least a four-three fit is found.

Here is an example of how well this escape system befuddles the opponents:

```
Dealer: N            ♠ K x
Vul.: Both           ♥ A x x
                     ♦ K x x x
                     ♣ Q J T x

♠ A x x                        ♠ T x x x
♥ K J T x          N           ♥ Q x x
♦ Q J T        W  ✧  E         ♦ A x x
♣ K x x            S           ♣ A x x

                     ♠ Q J x x
                     ♥ x x x
                     ♦ x x x
                     ♣ x x x
```

North	East	South	West
1NT	Pass	Pass	Double
Pass	Pass	2♠	Pass
3♣	Pass	Pass	?

Even though East-West together own 24 HCP, West is helpless in the pass-out seat. East-West do not know their actual strength. East does not know that her partner has 14 HCP while South has only 3. West could just as well have 9 while South has 8. Similarly, West does not know that his partner has 10 HCP. East could just as well have 5 while South has 8. Neither East nor West knows that their side has the combined strength either to make a lucrative penalty double or to bid their cold 3NT. Moreover, they cannot find out.

Consider East's and West's quandaries at each stage of the auction:

North	East	South	West
1NT	Pass	Pass	Double
Pass	?		

How can East come in here? Her only real possibility is 2NT, but that is much too risky if West has 11 or fewer HCP. So she passes:

North	East	South	West
1NT	Pass	Pass	Double
Pass	Pass	2♠	?

How can West re-enter the auction here? If East has a dog of a hand while South has even a 7-count with decent values in the black suits, East-West could be dead meat. So he passes too:

North	East	South	West
1NT	Pass	Pass	Double
Pass	Pass	2♠	Pass
3♣	?		

Now is East's last chance, but what can she do? She knows that North-South are in a Moysian fit, because South has told everyone his shape and North did not redouble at her first opportunity, which would have shown a five-card suit. But 3-level Moysian contracts often make. So there can be no double, either optional or penalty or otherwise. Can she bid her only other suit, spades, or NT, with South's four spades behind her? That's a rhetorical question. She has no reasonable choice but to pass.

East-West have been completely bamboozled by AWNT and its escape system. If North-South had been playing Standard American, East-West would easily have found 3NT, as follows:

North	East	South	West
1♦	Pass	Pass	1NT
Pass	2NT	Pass	3NT

West duly notes that East was unable to make either a bid or a takeout double, but — unless North is hiding a monster — also knows that she has some values, since South's pass pegged his hand at only 0-5 HCP. West's balancing 1NT shows 11-14 HCP, which East judges is worth her invitation to 3NT. West gladly accepts. The contract makes. North's natural lead is ♣Q. West wins in dummy, knocks out ♥A, wins the club return in hand, runs the hearts, and leads ♦Q, finishing with one spade, three hearts, three diamonds, and two clubs.

Here is one more instance of snookering the opponents with the Baldwinsville escape system:

```
Dealer: S        ♠ K x x x
Vul.: Both       ♥ K x x
                 ♦ Q x x
                 ♣ J x x

♠ A Q J              N           ♠ x x x
♥ x x x x                        ♥ A Q J
♦ x x x      W   ✧   E           ♦ J x x x x
♣ K x x              S           ♣ Q x

                 ♠ x x x
                 ♥ x x x
                 ♦ A K
                 ♣ A x x x x
```

South	West	North	East
1NT	Pass	Pass	Double
Redouble	Pass	Pass(!)	2♦
Pass	Pass	Pass	

North knows that her side has at least 20 HCP and an eight-card minor suit fit. She reasons that with her two half-stoppers in the majors, South will have plenty of time to establish and run this minor. So she wisely passes rather than continue the transfer. As captain and as the only member of the pair with sufficient information, responder in all cases is the only member of the pair who may convert either the opponents' double of the weak 1NT or partner's redouble to penalty.

East correctly surmises that South's five-card minor is clubs. She is not happy about bidding 2♦, but 1NT redoubled is game and she cannot risk that.

2♦ always makes, possibly with an overtrick, because the most that North-South can get is one spade, no hearts, three diamonds, and one club. So East-West gets either 90 or 110.

But the irony is that 1NT redoubled should go down! West leads a heart and East returns a diamond. South leads his fourth-best club and dummy's jack loses to East's queen. East continues diamonds. South continues clubs. West takes his king and continues hearts. East wins and, having noticed West's discouraging diamond signals, cashes ♥A (dropping North's king) and switches to a spade. West grabs the ace and cashes the long heart for down one. That would have been plus 400 for East-West.

A Standard American auction on this deal might have gone like this:

South	West	North	East
1♣	Pass	1♠	2♦
Pass	2NT	Pass	Pass
Pass			

North leads a spade. West starts the diamonds. South returns a spade. North wins the hook and no matter what she does, North-South can only ever get their one spade, three diamonds, and one club. East-West would have had 120, a very competitive matchpoint result.

After Overcalls

If your opening weak 1NT is overcalled, there is little to worry about. You have already escaped.

Nevertheless, you or your partner — the captain — might want to get back into the auction, believing that your best chance on this deal would be when your side declares rather than defends.

First of all, and this is most important, *whenever opener's 1NT is overcalled with a natural suit, responder's double is strictly for penalty.* Opener may take the double out if she wishes, but only if she realizes that she is risking partner's wrath. Responder is, after all, the captain.

This principle is a specific instance of a broader principle that applies to Standard American as well as K-S: *Whenever either our side or their side bids a natural NT at any level, any subsequent double by our side is for penalty.*

If the 1NT opening is overcalled with an artificial bid, say a Cappelletti 2♦ showing hearts and spades, responder should not double right away to indicate the ability to punish either hearts or spades. That would give the opponents too much information and partner not enough. Rather, responder should wait until advancer chooses a suit, then, on the second round, whack it if he can.

If the 1NT opening is overcalled with a natural suit, then any suit that responder bids either higher on the 2-level or at the 3-level follows the Lebensohl system. That is, responder's 2NT is an artificial relay to 3♣, after which responder will further define his hand. His cue bid of the enemy suit — not 3♣ — is Stayman. If the cue bid is direct, it is Stayman without a stopper (Fast Approach Denies Stopper = "FADS"), but if the 2NT - 3♣ relay occurs before the cue bid, it is Stayman with a stopper (Slow Approach Shows Stopper = "SASS"). Responder's new suit, including 3♣, bid directly at the 3-level is natural and forcing. If the new suit bid at the 3-level follows the 2NT - 3♣ relay, it is drop dead if lower ranking than the enemy suit but invitational if higher ranking. If responder wants to drop dead in a suit that ranks higher than the enemy suit, he just bids it directly at the 2-level.

Lebensohl is off when the overcall is artificial. This is tantamount to saying that it is hardly ever on anymore, as nowadays nearly all overcalls of NT openings are artificial, e.g., DONT, Cappelletti, Brozel, etc.

When opener's LHO overcalls an artificial bid such as Cappelletti, Brozel, or DONT, any new suit by responder is natural and to play. Responder's 2NT or 3NT in this situation shows stoppers in all the implied enemy suits, along with the appropriate HCP values.

Texas transfers are always on, whether the overcall is natural or artificial. They provide a great way to get back into the auction without allowing your opponents the opportunity to exchange any further information — unless they want to chime in at the 4-level.

If the opponents' suits are the majors, e.g., when their overcall is a Cappelletti 2♦, then responder's direct bid of 4♠ is MSS, promising no worse than five-five in the minors and — usually — drop dead values. But, after opener picks a minor at the 5-level, responder may blast to slam in that minor with exceptional controls and distribution, such as ♠— ♥x ♦AKxxxx ♣AKxxxx.

Adapting Escapes to Simple Bridge

A sizeable number of tournament and club players are fed up with today's complicated conventions, elaborate rules, and incoherent alert procedures. They wish to play just a simple, basic game of bridge. These players and their wishes must be respected. After all, we play bridge to have fun, not to create headaches for ourselves.

Plain old-fashioned bridge *is* fun! There is no doubt of that. But the trouble with it is that its bidding methods are just plain inferior to those of modern bridge. There is no doubt of that either.

Folks who prefer to play plain old-fashioned bridge still like to win, and they especially love to beat wild and crazy hotshots who play all those complicated conventions, elaborate rules, and incoherent alert procedures. But such victories do not happen very often — for the plain and simple reason that old-fashioned bidding is, well, inferior.

The ACBL created two special convention cards for players who prefer plain bridge: the ACBL Standard American Yellow Card (well known as just "SAYC") in 1988 and the ACBL Classic Card[2] in 1996. The SAYC has become quite popular, especially online. The Classic Card in its original form has fallen away, but it has evolved into the ACBL "Fat Free" Card, which is still a going concern in 2006. Both the SAYC and the Fat Free Card specifically disallow many of the more complicated conventions and treatments. The whole purpose of these convention cards is to simplify and streamline the game.

So the question is: Can enough of an AWNT system be legally included on a simple convention card to keep the game fun for the players of simple bridge but at the same time make them competitive against players of complex modern bidding methods?

---

[2] There is an excellent article on this topic in the November 1996 ACBL *Bulletin*: "Allowable Conventions for Classic Bridge" (pp. 75-79), including a sample ACBL classic bridge convention card.

The answer — like most answers to bridge questions — is a qualified yes and no.

The SAYC — being "Standard American" — allows only the opening 1NT range of 15-17 HCP. The Fat Free Card allows an opening 1NT range of not more than three HCP, with the low end not less than 11 and the high end not greater than 19 HCP. So far so good. We can play the weak NT (12-14 HCP) with the Fat Free Card but not with the SAYC.

But the Fat Free Card — true to its goal of keeping things easily manageable — would specifically disallow Lebensohl, ConFit, forcing Stayman, puppet Stayman, Bergen raises, funny raises, the Jacoby 2NT system, splinters, 1NT forcing, SSGT/PERR, inverted minors, mini-Roman, responsive doubles, Namyats and other transfer preempts, RKC, modified Roman Blackwood, and many other useful gadgets. Yet Cappelletti, Brozel, DONT, and other defensive overcall systems against NT openings seem to be allowed, as are Michaels cue bids and the unusual NT. Also, Jacoby transfers for the majors, Texas transfers, plain old Stayman, plain old Gerber, plain old Blackwood, strong 2♣, weak twos for the other three suits, and ultra-light overcalls and preempts are OK. In the "maybe / maybe not" category are MSS, the gambling 3NT, Jacoby steps, crazy steps, jump cue bids, and SOS redoubles, i.e., redoubles which serve no other purpose than to tell partner to run.

Those restrictions alone would not make AWNT unplayable on the Fat Free Card. But what about escapes? We need our escapes.

All the components of all the AWNT escape systems (ROS, transfer or Moscow escapes, and Baldwinsville escapes) are alertable. More than alertable, they are complicated, and so are anathema to Fat Free theory, which values friendliness above accuracy. Yet the Baldwinsville escape system is just an elaboration of plain old SOS redoubles, which Fat Free probably should allow; and the transfer escape system should be allowed if Jacoby transfers are allowed in competition, at least for the majors. As for the forcing pass that requires opener to redouble, we would probably have to give it up.

When in doubt, ask the director!

6

The Strong, Artificial, and Forcing 2♣ Opening

There are so few "monster" suited hands in bridge that using up four possible opening bids (i.e., natural 2♣, 2♦, 2♥, and 2♠) to show them makes little sense. These hands are now all typically shown artificially, e.g., with 2♣ in Standard American, Acol, and K-S, and with 1♣ in Precision and other "Big Club" systems as the strong, forcing bid. No serious bridge player uses strong, natural two bids anymore.

The greatest advantage of the strong, artificial, and forcing 2♣ opening is that it frees the 2♦, 2♥, and 2♠ opening bids for other purposes. Generally the major opening two bids are used for weak, one-suited pre-empts and the opening 2♦ is used either as a weak two or conventionally to show a multi-suited hand. These bids are discussed below in Chapters 7 and 8.

When to Open 2♣

There are — generally speaking — three traditional methods of evaluating a hand to determine whether it ought to be opened with a strong 2♣: (1) point count, (2) quick trick count, and (3) proximity to game.

1. Using point count as the criterion, many players will open 2♣ with 23+ HCP and a good five-card suit, 22+ HCP and a good six-card suit, or 21+ HCP and either a good seven-card suit or an extraordinary six-card suit. This highly disciplined method is too restrictive.

2. Many good players open 2♣ if they have at least 8½ quick tricks in hand. There is little to quarrel with this.

3. We often see "WOTOG" written on ACBL convention cards. That means "Within One Trick Of Game," or in other words, the hand contains eight tricks if game is envisioned in no trump, nine tricks if in a major, and ten tricks if in a minor. These tricks are not necessarily "quick," but should be fairly certain. Responder is expected to provide only about 3-4 HCP (i.e., approximately one trick) to the game effort.

All three of these methods also use the opening 2♣ to begin sequences that show hands with no trump distribution and HCP ranges in the twenties.

WOTOG is superior to the other two methods because it is more versatile. There are many highly distributional 14+ HCP hands that may not have 8½ quick tricks but still are within one trick of game and therefore should be opened 2♣. For example, ♠QT9875432 ♥— ♦AQ ♣AQ will surely make 4♠ with almost no help from partner. Most players would open that hand either 1♠, 4♠, or, artificially, 4♦,[1] but should have no qualms

---

[1] This choice depends on partnership agreement. See the discussions of

about opening it 2♣, especially since, to have a good chance at slam, responder needs as little as ♠Ax (to drop the opponents' singleton ♠K and ♠J, a 52% probability) and (assuming an entry to dummy) either a minor suit Kxx to pitch the other minor suit queen under the king or ♥AK to pitch both minor suit queens. Say that responder's hand is ♠AJ ♥J98542 ♦K75 ♣74. Three possible auctions are as follows, with the opponents passing throughout:

2♣	2♦ (waiting)
2♠ (natural)	3♠ (natural)
4♣ (cue bid first-round control)	4NT[2]
5♦[3]	6♦[4]
6♠ (to play)	

2♣	2♥ (constructive)
2♠ (natural)	3♠ (natural)
4♣ (cue bid first-round control)	4NT[2]
5♦[3]	6♦[4]
6♠ (to play)	

2♣	2♠[5]
3♠ (natural)	4NT[6]
5NT (two aces and a void)	6♠ (to play)

"Suit Openings at the 4-Level" and "Namyats" in Chapter 8.

[2] By partnership agreement, once a control-showing cue bid sequence is entered, 4NT cannot be Blackwood. Rather, it conventionally shows the trump ace, since any bid of the trump suit itself would be a signoff. This particular 4NT denies first-round control of the intervening suits, since control-showing cue bids are done up-the-line.

[3] Showing first-round control of diamonds, denying second-round control of clubs.

[4] Showing second-round control of diamonds, denying second-round control of the intervening suits.

[5] Artificial bid in the "Crazy Steps" system of responses to 2♣, showing exactly 9-10 HCP. For a full description of Crazy Steps, see the end of this chapter.

[6] Modified Roman Blackwood. See the full description in Chapter 13.

Using 2♣ as a prelude to rebid 2NT to show a flat 22-23 HCP or to rebid 3NT to show a flat 24-25 HCP also falls within WOTOG because these hands are almost always within one trick of game. Remember that in the AWNT system our partnership wants to be in game if it jointly has at least 24 HCP. Granted that, in 3NT, 12 opposite 12 HCP plays better than 22 opposite 2 or 24 opposite none, responder might want to consider very carefully before raising opener to game in this situation.

Responses to the Strong 2♣ Opening

The greatest danger of opening a strong, artificial, and forcing 2♣ is that the weaker hand may become declarer in no trump. A somewhat lesser danger is that a major suit contract will be declared from the wrong side. The best set of responses to 2♣ will be so constructed that these dangers are minimized.

The strong 2♣ opener should be captain of the auction, trying — without masterminding partner — to become declarer so that the strong hand will remain concealed. Above all, the system of responses should reduce the odds of responder having to be the first to bid no trump. Thus it is important for responder make a limit bid at the first opportunity. In this way, opener will quickly be able to assess the combined strength of the two hands. Opener needs information!

Using the 2♦ response as "waiting," i.e., as a simple relay for opener to further describe the strong hand, is a wasted bid. It tells the opener absolutely nothing. Opener needs to know responder's strength, but with a waiting bid, responder could have anywhere between zero and all the rest of the HCP in the deck. The purpose of this response is noble, i.e., to ensure that opener will be the first to bid a major suit or no trump, but its many disadvantages outweigh this one great advantage.

The "double negation" system is an improvement over the waiting 2♦. Responder bids 2♦ to show 0-6 HCP, then, by partnership agreement, rebids either 2NT or the cheaper minor as the second negative to show 0-3 HCP. Any other bid or rebid is constructive. These responses give good information, but not enough.

Increasingly popular at the beginning of the new millennium is the "heart bust" system of responses to 2♣. There are only four possible responses, all artificial:

2♦ = 3+ HCP, the only positive response.
2♥ = 0-3 HCP, usually a flat bust, but may include a long minor.
2♠ = drop-dead transfer to 3♥, very weak hand with at least six hearts.
2NT = drop-dead transfer to 3♠, very weak hand with at least six spades.

The big advantage of this system is that it provides a convenient mechanism to shut off the auction at a level below game if game seems hopeless. The disadvantage is that responder may be the first to bid NT. Yet this disadvantage, which is significant in other systems, is small in this system because, if responder has an ultra-weak hand with a long major, ending up in 3NT is quite unlikely.

Even better than waiting, double negation, or the heart bust system are the several species of step responses. Steps can show either HCP or the number of controls. Typically, controls are indicated in response to an opening 2♣ by counting an ace as two controls and a king as one.

One frequently encountered schedule of these control-showing step responses is:

2♦ = no controls, i.e., no aces or kings, with 0-4 HCP.

2♥ = one control, i.e., either precisely one king, or no kings with 5-8 HCP.

2♠ = two controls, i.e., either two kings, or one ace, or no kings or aces with 9-12 HCP.

2NT = three controls in the form of precisely three kings.

3♣ = three controls in the form of precisely one ace and one king.

3♦ = four controls.

3♥ = five controls.

3♠ = six controls.

3NT = seven or more controls, but it is unlikely that any hand responding to 2♣ would contain that many, i.e., a minimum of three kings and two aces. There are, after all, only twelve controls in the deck.

Traditional Jacoby Steps[7] are even better:

2♦ = 0-3 HCP

2♥ = 4-6 HCP

2♠ = 7-9 HCP

2NT = 10-12 HCP

3♣ = 13-15 HCP

3♦ = 16-18 HCP

3♥ = 19+ HCP

One advantage of the Jacoby Steps system is that it reduces the chances of responder being the first to bid NT. After all, it is rare for the partner of a strong 2♣ opener to hold as many as 10-12 HCP. Some pairs eliminate this problem by skipping the 2NT response, so:

2♦ = 0-3 HCP

2♥ = 4-6 HCP

2♠ = 7-9 HCP

3♣ = 10-12 HCP

---

[7] Invented by Oswald Jacoby and described by his son James Jacoby on pp. 46-49 of *Jacoby on Bridge* (New York: Pharos, 1987).

3♦ = 13-15 HCP
3♥ = 16-18 HCP
3♠ = 19+ HCP

Jacoby Steps provide a four-point range in the first step and a three-point range thereafter, which is too wide for some purposes in hand evaluation, particularly when making a borderline slam decision.

The most powerful set of responses to 2♣ is a tight variant of Jacoby Steps where the range of the first step is three points and the range of subsequent steps is only two:

2♦ = 0-2 HCP
2♥ = 7-8 HCP
2♠ = 9-10 HCP
2NT = 15-16 HCP
3♣ = 3-4 HCP
3♦ = 5-6 HCP
3♥ = 11-12 HCP
3♠ = 13-14 HCP
3NT = 17-18 HCP

They might be easier to remember if shown this way:

0-2 HCP = 2♦
3-4 HCP = 3♣
5-6 HCP = 3♦
7-8 HCP = 2♥
9-10 HCP = 2♠
11-12 HCP = 3♥
13-14 HCP = 3♠
15-16 HCP = 2NT
17-18 HCP = 3NT

You can call these "Crazy Steps", "Syracuse Steps," or even "Luft Steps," since I made them up. Their most important advantage is that the most harmless bids are used for the most common responses. The extra bidding space that Crazy Steps take up is well worthwhile.

Say you open 2♣ with ♠AKJTxxxx ♥KJTx ♦A ♣—. That is only 16 HCP, but you are a cinch for game and only about half a trick short of slam. You do not need much from partner at all. You could not care less what she has in the minors, or even spades, but you would love for her to have ♥A or at least ♥Q. How can you find out? Playing Crazy Steps, partner might bid 2♦ to show 0-2 HCP, but if that includes ♥Q, then you definitely want to play in 6♠. Again, how can you find out?

The answer to this difficult question lies in the duty of responder to provide opener with as much descriptive information as possible. After 2♣-2♦-2♠, there remains plenty of bidding space to do this. Responder's first obligation is to support opener's suit if possible, second obligation to avoid bidding NT unless absolutely necessary, and third obligation to show long suits or good suits. Some helpful rebids by responder in this auction would be: 3♣ with x-xxxx-xxxx-xxxx, 3♦ with x-xxxx-xxxxx-xxx, or 3♥ with x-Qxx-xxxxx-xxxx.

None of this is foolproof, and opener may never be able to determine whether 6♥ is a safe bid, but at least responder will have done everything possible in the auction. Responder must always be thinking about how to help opener, the captain, know what to do.

Using any of these response systems, if 2♣ is over-called, responder may double for penalty, pass to show 0-4 HCP, bid a natural suit to show 5+ HCP without a stopper, bid NT to show 5+ HCP with a stopper in the opponents' suit, or cue bid that suit to ask for a stopper.

The so-called "stiff king problem" always remains. If opener holds Ax or Qx opposite responder's singleton king, then that king is working; but if opener holds the stiff ace or a small doubleton in that suit, then the king is worthless. How is responder to know? There is no easy answer. Probably the best strategy is for responder to show the king as a control or to show its 3 HCP (depending on the response system) and just hope that all goes well.

7

The Mini-Roman 2◊ Opening

Among the world's worst conventions must be Flannery. It gives up a lot and gains nothing. It tells the opponents just about everything they need to know to defend the hand, and — even worse — it is completely unnecessary. If we play the 1NT forcing response to the 1♥ opening, *we will find the four-four spade fit if it exists*, because responding 1NT to 1♥ is an absolute 100% positive strike-me-dead-if-I'm-lying-or-mistaken denial that there are as many as four spades in responder's hand!

So we never play Flannery, anytime, anywhere, with any partner! What, then, can we do with the 2♦ opening?

We could play it as a standard weak two bid, but a natural minor suit opening at the two level does not have much preemptive value, since both majors are still readily available to the opponents. With a hand that we could theoretically open a weak 2♦, it is probably better in most cases to either open 3♦ or pass.

The Mini-Roman 2♦ opening (also known as Modified Roman 2♦ because the original Roman 2♦

showed 17-20 HCP) is completely artificial and disciplined. It shows 11-15 HCP, an undisclosed singleton or void, and either 4-4-4-1 or 4-4-5-0 distribution with no five-card major. It says nothing about diamonds.

If responder's RHO passes, responder may not pass, since opener could be void in diamonds. If responder's RHO doubles for whatever reason, then responder should pass. If responder's LHO also passes the double, then opener will rebid the hand's shortness, thus giving responder all the information necessary to establish the final contract.

If responder is interested in game, then, after her RHO's pass, she bids 2NT as a relay, asking opener to bid his short suit at the 3-level. The 2NT bid is completely artificial and says nothing about no trump. After opener names the short suit, responder has enough information to establish the contract with her second bid, which opener must pass.

If responder does not have the values opposite opener's 11-15 HCP to explore for game, then she just starts bidding playable suits up the line until the partnership finds at least a four-four fit. This is a very simple process. Say responder bids 2♥ and opener passes. Responder then knows that opener has exactly four hearts, and will expect to declare that contract unless the opponents get into the auction. Say opener does not pass responder's 2♥. Responder then knows that opener's shortness is in hearts. She can use her second bid to select the contract, which opener must pass.

The partner of the Mini-Roman 2♦ opener is *always and forever* the captain of the auction.

Mini-Roman hands occur much more often than Flannery hands. There are only five possible Flannery shapes: 4♠-5♥-0♦-4♣, 4♠-5♥-4♦-0♣, 4♠-5♥-3♦-1♣, 4♠-5♥-1♦-3♣, and 4♠-5♥-2♦-2♣; but ten possible Mini-Roman shapes: 4♠-4♥-0♦-5♣, 4♠-4♥-5♦-0♣, 4♠-4♥-1♦-4♣, 4♠-4♥-4♦-1♣, 4♠-0♥-5♦-4♣, 4♠-0♥-4♦-5♣, 4♠-1♥-4♦-4♣, 0♠-4♥-5♦-4♣, 0♠-4♥-4♦-5♣, and 1♠-4♥-4♦-4♣.

One of the most profitable aspects of this bid is that it will often throw non-expert opponents into a tizzy. Even with a full opening hand, and even after opener's partner has explained the bid and suggested defenses to it, the LHO of the Mini-Roman 2♦ opener may be reluctant to enter the auction, or may enter it incorrectly, or may enter it correctly only to have partner interpret it incorrectly.[1]

Consider the tactical advantage for East using Mini-Roman on this deal:

```
Dealer: E        ♠ J 8 4
Vul.: Both       ♥ 3 2
                 ♦ K 8 7 6
                 ♣ A Q T 5

 ♠ Q 3                          ♠ A
 ♥ A Q T 6          N           ♥ 9 8 7 5
 ♦ T 5 3       W   ✧   E        ♦ A Q 9 4
 ♣ 9 6 3 2          S           ♣ J 8 7 4

                 ♠ K T 9 7 6 5 2
                 ♥ K J 4
                 ♦ J 2
                 ♣ K
```

South would have a problem if East passed. There are legitimate reasons for opening that hand either 1♠ (enough HCP) or 2♠ (too strong for 3-level preempt) or 3♠ (no defensive values). Such borderline hands are

---

[1] I recall a deal in the Swiss teams at the Rochester Sectional, neither side vulnerable, when my partner opened 2♦ with a 15-count and 4-1-4-4 distribution. My RHO overcalled a natural 3♦ with a long suit and a weak hand. I passed with my flat 4-count. Even after I answered LHO's request for a thorough explanation of the Mini-Roman convention, she misinterpreted her partner's call as a cue bid and was off to the races. By the time they stumbled into 4♠ on a seven-card fit, our side was happy to double for a three-trick set of 500 points and a swing of 12 IMPs.

often helped if they are allowed to overcall rather than obligated to open.

The natural opening for East is 1♦. That would solve South's problem immediately, since a simple overcall of 1♠ would give North a clear enough picture for the first round of bidding. The auction would become a duel between spades and hearts for the partial score, with 3♥ making and with 3♠ going down one as long as the defenders could cash four red suit winners before clubs were broken.

But if East opens a Mini-Roman 2♦, South's original problem just becomes worse. If South (1) passes, West will be free to follow the system unhindered (in this case with a run-out bid of 2♥); (2) bids 2♠, North will not have a clear idea of South's strength; (3) bids 3♠, South understates the strength of the hand; (4) bids 4♠, South masterminds the auction (in this case dumping the pair into an unmakeable contract).

Critics of Mini-Roman 2♦ say that it gives the opponents too much information and guides their defense to the detriment of declarer. There is some truth in this — but not a lot. Opener almost always becomes dummy in a Mini-Roman auction, so declarer's hand remains a mystery for defenders to solve.

8

Opening Preempts

One of the main advantages of any aggressive system is that it gives you more opportunities to interfere with the opponents' auction when they own the deal, to start their auction at the 2-level and higher, and thus to rob them of the luxury of ample bidding space. With AWNT, besides being able to open 1NT more often, you have expanded prospects for using preemptive suit bids. Preempt whenever possible, and do it without fear. You will take a big loss once in a while, but in the long run wild preempting is a winning strategy. Bridge is a bidder's game.

Here are a few general principles of preempting. Partner must be able to trust you implicitly. While we are undisciplined about point count, suit length, and suit quality, especially non-vulnerable vs. vulnerable, we must, for the partnership's sake, be absolutely disciplined about two aspects of the preempting hand:

1. It must not contain an outside four-card or longer major.
2. It must not contain a void.

Our objective is to preempt the opponents, not partner. We do not want to miss finding a major suit fit if we have it; so, if partner is an unpassed hand, your opening preempt absolutely guarantees that you do not have as many as four cards in either major, unless that major is the preempting suit. This restriction against having an outside four-card major may be relaxed when partner is a passed hand, because, by that stage in the auction, finding a major suit fit has become less important for your side.

Here are just four good reasons not to open a preempt when holding a void:

1. Your hand is too strong. A void is worth five distributional points and is probably undervalued at that. A void has so many positive offensive characteristics that they should not be lost to the auction by your advertising that you have a weak hand. Among these characteristics might lie the difference between declaring and defending. Do not fool partner into believing that you do not have a void when you really do. Above all, you do not want partner to decide — on the basis of your preempt, which led her to the false belief that you had no void — to defend rather than bid the cold game in your suit.

2. If partner, the captain, has a void in your suit or for any other reason judges that bailing out is the best tactic in a particular situation, she can bid a non-forcing new suit as a sign-off with the assurance that you will not be void in that suit.

3. If you pass rather than either preempt or overcall your suit when you have a void, especially when partner is a passed hand, then you will contribute toward hiding the actual distribution of the deal from the opponents. True, they will not expect you to have a void if you preempt, but, by your passing, they will not expect you to have a long suit either. Few facts about defenders' hands are more discon-

certing for declarer than bad splits, especially when declarer discovers them unexpectedly. So keep such facts hidden as long as possible, to surprise the opponents at the most inopportune time for them.

4. Whether partner is a passed hand or not, if you pass rather than preempt, you will almost certainly get another chance to bid, if you wish. Your pass does not shut either you yourself or your side out of the auction.

Never relax the restriction against opening a preempt with a void in your hand!

Weak Two Bids

The best advice I ever got concerning weak two bids was to play them undisciplined at matchpoints, especially non-vulnerable. This advice came to me second-hand from a number of partners, but I think that its ultimate source must be Marty Bergen.

The weak two bid is — along with the weak 1NT opening itself — one of the most powerful and profitable aspects of the AWNT system. Especially if your suit is spades, you have the luxury of forcing the opponents to begin their auction at either 2NT or the 3-level. Unless one of them has 16+ HCP, you might just shut them out of the auction completely. Because of its gigantic preemptive value, you would do very well to maximize the number of times when you are able to make a weak two bid. That means relaxing the requirements.

Besides having no requirements about a six-card suit, let's have none of that hidebound two-of-the-top-three-honors nonsense either. Paying attention to suit quality when contemplating opening a non-vulnerable

weak two will only stifle your game. Open jack-high
fifth non-vulnerable vs. vulnerable if partner can stand
it. Just make absolutely sure that you have *fully* discussed this style with partner first.[1]

Of course, if you are going to play weak twos
wild and undisciplined — and reap the benefits there-
from — you will need some kind of mechanism to protect yourself and partner from a big set. The standard
method of using the 2NT response as feature-asking
just will not work if you are not adhering strictly to
six-card suits with two of the top three honors. Responder, the captain, will have to know more about both
your suit quality and your hand quality in order to
make an intelligent decision.

The strong warning above in Chapter 1 that responder must be disciplined if opener is wild applies especially to weak two bids. If you do not follow this advice, you and your partner are dead meat!

Since a non-vulnerable weak two bid in AWNT
can be made with as little as a five-card honorless major in a wimpy 5-HCP hand,[2] responder must absolutely have a *minimum* of 16 HCP to make a 2NT con-

---

[1] I cannot overemphasize the importance of making absolutely sure that
you and partner understand and appreciate each other's style before you
sit down to play. At the 1993 Syracuse Regional, we lost a Swiss team
match because my partner assumed that my 2♠ opening showed two of
the top three honors. She blasted to 6♠ — which would have been
exactly the right bid if I had had what she thought I had. In fact I had
JT9xxx (non-vulnerable vs. vulnerable) with ♣AQ, and the contract
went down like a rock. At the other table, 4♠ made five for a swing of
11 IMPs. So, unless you are going to play nothing but Stone Age
Goren, talk to partner about every little thing first!

[2] Marty Bergen and Larry Cohen were having such wonderful success
with wildly undisciplined weak two bids that the ACBL changed the
rules at the 1984 San Antonio Spring North American Bridge Champi-
onships specifically in order to rein them in. Known as "The Marty
Bergen Rule," it states that any weak two bid must show at least 5 HCP
and at least a five-card suit.

structive bid. That guarantees that the pair will have at least 21 HCP at the 3-level. If responder cannot be comfortable with that, then she should not bid 2NT. With less than 16 HCP, she can either raise the pre-empt, usually to the 3-level after a takeout double, raise to game expecting to make, or pass. Bidding a new suit is hardly ever a good idea. It is better to trap pass and let the opponents either bid that suit them-selves or discover the adverse distribution after they have declared in some third suit or in NT.

Rather than feature-asking, using 2NT as Ogust is a step in the right direction toward the captain being able to gather the maximum of helpful information from the weak two opener. After a forcing 2NT response from partner, and nothing but passes from the opposi-tion, opener rebids 3♣ to show a bad hand with a bad suit, 3♦ to show a bad hand with a good suit, 3♥ to show a good hand with a bad suit, 3♠ to show a good hand with a good suit, and 3NT to show a solid suit (minimum AKQxxx). By partnership agreement, the meanings of the 3♦ and 3♥ rebids may be reversed, but I always find that terribly confusing.

A far superior method is one that I learned from world champion Jeff Meckstroth at the 1994 Ottawa Regional,[3] called "WoJust" — or "Walter Johnson's Ogust."[4] Following the 2NT forcing response, opener's

---

[3] By all means, no matter how good you think you are, *attend* the novice lectures given by world class experts at regionals and nationals. These players are amazing, and you will almost always learn something useful when they are just speaking off the cuff. Meckstroth taught WoJust to our group in response to the question: "Do you think that feature-showing or Ogust is the superior method with weak two bids?"

[4] Walter Johnson, playing with Eric Rodwell, won the Blue Ribbon Pairs in 1985 and, as a member of Rodwell's and Meckstroth's team, the Grand National Teams in 1990. His weak two response method is also described, but not specifically named, by Ron Andersen and Sabine Zenkel in *Preempts from A to Z* (Stamford, Connecticut: Magnus Books, 1993), pp. 36-39. Andersen and Zenkel attribute it to Meck-

possible rebids are:

   3♣ = five-card suit, any strength
   3♦ = six-card suit with about 5-6 HCP
   3♥ = six-card suit with about 7-8 HCP
   3♠ = six-card suit with about 9-10 HCP
   3NT = solid six-card suit (minimum AKQxxx)

   The guidelines for showing minimum, medium, or maximum hand strength in HCP are not rigid. For instance, a good 7 HCP hand often plays better than a bad 9 HCP hand, and opener should adjust the rebids accordingly. Certainly ♠AKxxxx ♥x ♦xxx ♣xxx plays better than ♠xxxxxx ♥QJ ♦Kxx ♣Kxx, even though their preemptive values are the same. The captain wants to know about opener's playing strength. HCP are often a good indication of that, but not always. Using WoJust, opener should rebid 3♥ with the first of these hands, but 3♦ with the second.

   Responder's rebid of 3♦ after opener's rebid of 3♣ is artificial, asking about the playing strength of the hand with the five-card suit. Opener's second rebids then are:

   3♥ = five-card suit with about 5-6 HCP
   3♠ = five-card suit with about 7-8 HCP
   3NT = five-card suit with about 9-10 HCP

That's the whole WoJust system. It's beautiful because it conveys maximum information while providing maximum safety.

   Weak two bids in fourth seat have no preemptive value; therefore they should not be made, at least not with our usual 5-10 HCP range. Obeying the Rule of 15 — which says to let the deal pass out unless your

---

stroth and Rodwell — "Meck-Well" — but in Ottawa Meckstroth attributed it to Johnson.

hand contains enough spades and enough HCP to add up to 15 or more — opening 2♥ in fourth seat shows a five-card or longer suit and 11-14 HCP, while opening 2♠ shows 10-14 HCP. By implication, then, opening 1♥ or 1♠ in fourth seat would show 15+ HCP.

Suit Openings at the 3-level

Since there is no such thing as a weak two bid in either minor in our system, these hands must be opened at the 3-level. That is just as well. An opening 2♣ or 2♦ — or even 2♥ if the opponents' suit is spades — does not have much preemptive value. But the 3-level! Ahh! That's where we really start disrupting the opponents!

At the 3-level and higher, the Rule of Two, Three and Four should come into consideration. Do not be afraid to open a lousy six-card or even sometimes a slightly better five-card suit at the 3-level, but always first do the calculations according to this rule.

At favorable vulnerability — which is when we have most of our fun! — hands such as ♠x ♥xxx ♦Qxx ♣KJxxxx or ♠x ♥xxx ♦AKJxx ♣xxxx qualify to be opened at the 3-level, but hands such as ♠K ♥QJ ♦Kxxxxx ♣xxxx or ♠Qx ♥Jxx ♦Kxx ♣Qxxxx do not. Neither of the first two is likely to go down more than four, counting three-and-a-half club tricks, half a diamond trick, and one trick from partner in the first hand; and four diamond tricks and one trick from partner in the second hand. We can almost always count on one trick from partner. But neither of the last two hands is likely to take more than two or three tricks, even with help from partner.

Responses are few. The most common and often the most useful is just to up the preempt to the 4-level, especially after opener's LHO has doubled in direct seat. Such obstructive raises can be made on no points and as few as two pieces of trump. They frustrate opener's RHO no end! Even if the doubler is four-four in the majors, as the double promises, doubler's partner does not have a clear fix on whether their side can make game — and now has no room left to find out. Taking the double out at 3♥ or 3♠ would have been comfortable with, say, 9 HCP, but now having to bid at the 4-level is dicey. If the doubler has 15 HCP, then the side wants to be in game, but if only 12 or 13, then probably not. How is doubler's partner to know?

After your opening 3-bid, a new suit bid by responder, in either a competitive or an uncontested auction, is non-forcing. If she wants to force you, she can cue bid the enemy suit in a competitive auction or bid 4NT (Blackwood) in an uncontested auction. Her bid of 3NT is to play. She is the captain; she knows things that you do not.

Suit Openings at the 4-level

The best aspect of 4-level opening preempts is that they steal 3NT from the opponents. That alone is a great reason to open what would normally be a 3-level preempt at the 4-level, especially in third seat. Again, use the Rule of Two, Three, and Four to determine whether to do this.

This section concerns only opening 4-level bids in the minors. We will take up the case of 4-level major suit openings in the next section, because, given that those preempts are game bids, special considerations apply to the majors.

Marty Bergen is renowned for saying "points

schmoints!" to express his contempt for HCP, suit quality, and other standard requirements to open or overcall preempts. But he himself attributes this catch-
phrase to Dorothy Hayden Truscott.[5] I already had
plenty of respect for Dorothy Truscott when I learned
that, but afterwards I had even more respect for her.
The following deal illustrates the sound principles that
underlie the whole "points schmoints!" attitude toward
bidding:

```
Dealer: N        ♠ K x x x
Vul.: E-W        ♥ K x x x
                 ♦ J x x x
                 ♣ K

♠ Q J T 9              N         ♠ A x x x
♥ A Q J T                        ♥ 9 x x x
♦ A K Q        W    ◇    E       ♦ T 9 x
♣ J T                 S          ♣ A Q

                 ♠ x
                 ♥ x
                 ♦ x x x
                 ♣ 9 x x x x x x x
```

South's shapely yarborough meets the Rule of Two,
Three, and Four. With eight clubs, he can reasonably
expect none of the other three hands to have more
than two. Therefore, after losing two tricks to crashing
honors, he would take six club tricks. Down four. Moreover, after two passes West is already marked with a
huge hand, possibly a 2♣ opener. That last little fact
makes South's preempt almost imperative. South is obligated to try to prevent the opponents from having an
easy road to their best contract. So he fearlessly and
confidently opens 4♣.

---

[5] Marty Bergen, *Better Bidding With Bergen, Volume One: Uncontested
Auctions* (Las Vegas: Max Hardy, 1985), p. 120.

But does South feel free to preempt just because North is a passed hand? That indeed helps, but what if East were the dealer? Should South preempt not knowing whether North would be a passed hand?

Again the Rule of Two, Three, and Four must be South's guide. Down four says "Bid." So South opens 4♣, even without knowing anything about partner's hand. How is West going to start to try to find their cold 6NT now?

Namyats

Namyats is another important protective measure for wild preempters. Sam Stayman invented it, but could not name it after himself because his usual partner, George Rapée, had already invented and named after Sam the popular conventional response to NT openings that we all know as "Stayman." So Stayman named his new convention "Namyats," which is just "Stayman" spelled backward. The two conventions have no systematic relation to each other.

Namyats solves a common problem with 4-level major suit openings. Sometimes we open a major at the 4-level solely to preempt, without a reasonable expectation of making the game. Other times we open a major at the 4-level with a slightly stronger hand, not quite strong enough to open at the 1-level by the Rule of 20, but still strong enough so that we expect to make the game. How is partner to know the difference?

Consider these spade hands:

1. ♠QJTxxxxx ♥xx ♦x ♣xx adds up to only 13 by the
   Rule of 20 and should be opened 4♠.
2. ♠AKJTxxxx ♥x ♦x ♣xxx adds up to 19 by the Rule of

20 and also should be opened 4♠.
   3. ♠AKJTxxxx ♥x ♦Kx ♣xx adds up to 21 by the Rule
   of 20 and should be opened 1♠.
   4. ♠AKJTxxxx ♥A ♦KQx ♣x is a monster that should
   be opened 2♣.

Hands 3 and 4 are not problematic, but Hand 1, which
will likely go down at 4♠, and Hand 2, which will
almost certainly make 4♠, illustrate the need for some
systematic way for responder to be able to tell them
apart. This is what Namyats does.

Namyats is a transfer preempt system in which
weaker preempts are opened directly and stronger
ones are opened in another suit. So, open Hand 1 4♠
and analogous heart hands 4♥, but open Hand 2 4♦
and analogous heart hands 4♣. Opening one of these
minors at the 4-level tells partner that you hold the
corresponding major in a hand that falls just short of a
1-level opening by the Rule of 20. With such a clear
picture of your hand, partner, the captain, will know
exactly what to do.

After your opening of 4♣ or 4♦, if partner believes
that slam is not possible, then she just completes the
transfer and declares game in your suit. If she bids the
intervening suit, that retransfers the suit back to you,
expressing her desire that you complete the transfer
and become declarer yourself. Any other bid she might
make indicates her slam interest. That would be either
4NT (Blackwood) or a cue bid of first-control in a suit
at the cheapest level above game in your suit. Also,
she might initiate slam exploration after you complete
the retransfer.

In *Modern Bridge Conventions*, pp. 177-178, Root
and Pavlicek suggest a cogent defense against Namyats. A double of the artificial minor is for takeout, with
shortness in the intended major and adequate support
for each of the other three suits. Other bridge players
prefer to use this double as lead directing, but since

that ploy can easily be stifled by the retransfer maneuver, Root's and Pavlicek's idea seems to be more theoretically sound. They also say that a double of the major itself is optional; that a direct cue bid of the intended major, before the opening side has had time to bid it, is a takeout for the other major and an undisclosed minor; that 4NT is a takeout for the minors; and that any other bid is natural. To this I would only add that some meaning should be assigned to a direct cue bid of the artificial minor, perhaps to show at least one-and-a-half controls in the intended major and expressing a desire for the overcalling side to declare 4NT if advancer, acting on this information, is willing to bid it. If this cue bid agreement is adopted as part of the defense, then, to show the artificial minor as a natural suit, overcaller would have to wait to bid until the transfer or retransfer has been completed.

9

Doubles! Doubles! Doubles!

The double was originally designed for penalty, but ever since around 1912, when an unknown auction bridge player made the first non-penalty double, its conventional meanings have relentlessly expanded in both number and complexity.

The double is one of our most useful and versatile calls. Its main advantage is that it does not take up any of our bidding space. Its main disadvantage is it does not take up any of the opponents' bidding space either.

Takeout Doubles

Because a takeout double uses none of the opponents' bidding space — and indeed since it gives the opponents some opportunities that would not have come to them if we had passed — we should be very disciplined about our takeout doubles. In direct seat we should prefer to overcall rather than double the opening bid for takeout, but if we have no suit to overcall, then we must let our hand, not our feelings, dictate our takeout double.

Four conditions above all must apply:

1. You must have a solid opening hand. No shading.
2. If RHO has opened a major, then your takeout double absolutely 100% promises exactly four cards in the other major — *except* when you are planning to rebid your own suit (major or minor) in the second round to show a 16+ HCP hand with one big, strong suit.
3. If RHO has opened a minor, then your takeout double promises either seven or eight cards in the majors: ideally four-four, but perhaps four-three, never four-two or three-three — again *except* when you have a 16+ HCP hand with one big, strong suit.
4. Last but not least, you must have the right shape. Never more than three cards in opener's suit and usually no more than two. *Do not make off-shape takeout doubles!*

So much for our side's takeout doubles. But what do we do when the opponents make one? How can we salvage our auction and disrupt theirs?

Your first obligation as responder is to let partner know which side owns the deal. After RHO doubles your partner's opening 1-level bid, you and LHO are the only players at the table who know which side owns the deal. All that RHO and your partner know so far is that the other has an opening hand. If partner has opened an 11-count, and if you have at least 10 HCP, then your side has at least 21. That's a majority. You own the deal. That's good news. In fact, that's great news! Tell your partner right away! Redouble! It shows

10+ HCP but gives no other message at all. It says nothing about fit, stoppers, controls, shape, or anything else. Just raw power. Any other call you make in this situation shows 0-9 HCP.

If you cannot redouble, then you must assume that the opponents own the deal. Your thinking now must focus on how to keep them from finding their best contract. The Principle of Fast Arrival should come immediately to mind. Either jump in partner's suit if you have a decent raise or jump in a new suit with at least six pieces. This weak jump shift applies even if partner has opened a major. Funny raises, Bergen raises, Jacoby raises, and all the rest of the major suit response systems are off in competition.

If your hand is too weak for a redouble and not shapely enough for either a jump raise or a jump shift, three possibilities remain:

Pass with 0-5 HCP.
Bid 1NT with 6-9 HCP, no more than two small cards in partner's suit, and with high cards — ideally stoppers — in each of the other three suits, i.e., doubler's implied suits.
Bid a new suit at the cheapest level with 6-9 HCP. This bid is forcing for one round, so be sure that you can stand whatever partner might rebid.

Negative Doubles

When is a third seat double after two bids negative and when is it penalty? When either first or second seat has bid a natural NT it is always penalty. When first seat has opened above the 1-level it is penalty. When second seat has overcalled at any level higher than the

first-and-third seats' partnership agreement (in our
case 3♠) it is penalty. When second seat has overcalled
with a conventional NT the third-seat double is also
conventional. In any other situation it is negative.

The negative double is an excellent weapon. It occurs frequently, performs its assigned tasks well, and
relinquishes little. It is especially useful in assisting a
partnership to define its major suit holdings precisely
at a low level, and thereby to bid confidently and effectively in a contested auction.

One very important point: Whenever you are in a
position to make a negative double, but bid a new suit
instead, you absolutely, positively, no-doubt-about-it
promise at least five cards in that suit — *never four.* If
you bid the cheapest number of bananas after partner
opens 1 grapefruit and the opponent in direct seat
overcalls oranges, then partner confidently knows that
you have at least five bananas, and can then act accordingly. If you had instead made a negative double,
you might have four bananas in a hand strong enough
to bid at that level, or you might have five or more
bananas in a hand too weak to bid at that level.

There are two schools of thought about making
negative doubles on weak hands with great shape: one
says, "Do it," the other says, "Pass." The answer is, of
course, like most answers in bridge: "It depends." But
on what does it depend? In AWNT, generally speaking,
if partner has opened a major, make the negative double, but if she has opened a minor, pass. That is
because, when we open a major, we are generally
aiming to play in that major, and only want to learn
how high to establish the contract. Your negative double will let partner know immediately that you do not
have as many as three cards in her suit. But when we
open a minor, we are usually aiming to end up somewhere else. As responder, tend to wait to get some indication of where opener wants to end up before you
give the opponents too much information.

Opening one of a minor in the AWNT system, there are only five kinds of hands that partner could have: 11-15 HCP one-suited, shown by rebidding the minor at the 2-level; 16+ HCP one-suited, shown by jump rebidding the minor; 15-17 HCP NT, shown by the variety of methods described above in Chapter 4; 18-19 HCP NT, shown by rebidding 2NT; or a hand containing a four-card major that does not qualify to be bid as NT. The point is that whenever partner opens a minor at the 1-level, you, as responder, will always get at least two chances to bid, and therefore can always feel free to pass the first round even with shortness in opener's minor. So, in this situation, if you do not have a suit, a legitimate NT response, or the exact shape to justify making a negative double, don't force it. Just pass and wait.

On rare occasions opener might convert responder's negative double to penalty. This conversion is more likely when the opponents are vulnerable and the overcall is at the 2-level. An example would be when opener has strong values, a poor fit for either of responder's suits, and a stack of trumps. Say partner's hand is ♠AKJxx ♥AQJxx ♦x ♣xx. She opens 1♠, RHO overcalls 2♥, and you make a negative double. Applying the formula for Klinger doubles described later in this chapter, she converts and your side reaps a nice reward.

Responsive Doubles

When LHO opens either 1 or 2 natural bananas, partner doubles for takeout, and RHO raises to either 2 or 3 bananas, then your double is responsive. It tells partner that you have competitive values, an inability to bid NT, more or less equal support in the three unbid suits, and no five-card or longer major. It demands that partner pick a suit to play if LHO passes on his second turn to bid. Accordingly you, the responsive doubler, should have no three-card suit in your hand. This last requirement is to prevent partner, the original doubler, from choosing what might turn out to be a Moysian fit.

If LHO has opened a major, then partner's takeout double promises exactly four cards in the other major and your responsive double likewise promises exactly four in that major. This is extremely useful information.

If LHO has opened a minor, then partner's takeout double promises no worse than four-three shape in the majors and tends to show four-four. You, however, as responsive doubler, should have precisely four-four in the majors. If you had four-three, then you would not make a responsive double, but would take partner out in your longer major, assuming, as you must, that his majors are four-four.

Say LHO opens 1♥. Partner overcalls 1NT. RHO raises to 2♥. What would your double mean then? Partner must hold no worse than ♥Kx or ♥Qxx for the announced stopper. RHO, freely competing behind the equivalent of a strong 1NT opener, is marked with good hearts (probably no worse than ♥Axx or ♥Kxxx) and some playing strength. You could not possibly have more than 8 HCP, assuming bare minimums for everyone else: LHO, 11; partner, 15; RHO, 6. Probably you are even weaker, and assuredly have short, weak hearts. Moreover, RHO seems unconcerned about partner's hearts. What then could there be in your hand which, when combined with partner's holding, could penalize the opponents? Precious little!

Thus your double must be a species of responsive double, asking partner to take out any of the three unbid suits. Partner has advertised a balanced hand, presumably with decent stuff outside the heart suit. The whole deal might be like this:

```
Dealer: N        ♠ K x x
Vul.: E-W        ♥ Q J x x x
                 ♦ x
                 ♣ K Q J x

♠ A x x x              N        ♠ Q J x
♥ —                            ♥ K x x
♦ T x x x        W   ✧   E     ♦ A K x x
♣ x x x x x            S        ♣ A x x

                 ♠ T x x
                 ♥ A T x x x
                 ♦ Q J x x
                 ♣ T
```

You perceive no problem for a 2♥ contract on this auction. Indeed in this case it should make three, losing just two spades, a diamond, and a club. So your double must be for takeout, denying a biddable suit and a five-card major, but offering partner the choice of three safe places to play at the 2 or 3-level. Do not worry that you only have 4 HCP. Your shape makes up for that deficiency. Moreover, partner already knows that you have a weak hand. He will easily figure out that your double is a three-suited takeout, not penalty. He may sometimes still rebid 2NT, or even in some rare instances leave the double in for penalty, but for this deal his rebid of 3♦ would be wisest. That contract goes down one, winning only two spades, three heart ruffs, two diamonds, and a club; but it will not be doubled, and -100 vulnerable is a good score compared to a field of -140s.

But say that in this auction RHO bids 3♥ instead of 2♥. Most systems would use that jump as a preemptive raise, denying any kind of playing strength. What would your double now mean? Perhaps the deal looks like this:

Dealer: N   ♠ K x x
Vul.: E-W   ♥ Q J x x x
              ♦ x
              ♣ K Q J x

♠ A J T x   ♠ Q x x
♥ —   N   ♥ A T
♦ Q J T x x W ✧ E   ♦ A K x x
♣ T x x x   S   ♣ A x x x

              ♠ x x x
              ♥ K x x x x x
              ♦ x x x
              ♣ x

Your double is now optional between responsive and penalty. You figure a minimum of 23 HCP on defense (your 8 plus partner's assumed 15). Partner can take the double out if he believes that your side would get a better result playing in one of your implied suits than on defense against a ten or eleven-card major-suit fit.

What if this were the deal?

Dealer: N   ♠ K x x
Vul.: E-W   ♥ Q J x x x
              ♦ x
              ♣ K Q J x

♠ A J T x   ♠ Q x x
♥ —   N   ♥ A K
♦ K Q J T   W ✧ E   ♦ A x x x
♣ T x x x x   S   ♣ A x x x

              ♠ x x x
              ♥ x x x x x x
              ♦ x x x x
              ♣ —

With a void and a known eleven-card major suit fit, third seat would surely raise to 4♥ on that yarborough.

Sitting with a full opener after three bids, and opposite a minimum of 15 HCP, fourth seat is not interested in either a partial score or a small set, but wants either a game or a big juicy set. But a big set is unlikely against the trump length that North-South have announced. There is not enough room for a cue bid. Moreover, if third seat's bid is 4♥, that takes away both the 3NT game, which is cold, and the possibility of a responsive double, which we play only up to 3♠. Fourth seat has a real problem.

Fourth seat is a captain of that pair, since second seat has made a limit bid. Fourth seat should not pass, but should keep the auction alive by informing partner somehow that third seat has either a yarborough or a very-near-yarborough. It is a *very* tough problem. That's why people preempt!

Consider a case in which you have 8 HCP and anticipate making a responsive double after partner doubles LHO's opening bid, but, instead of raising LHO's suit, RHO foils your plan by redoubling to show 10+ HCP. What then? You have already learned a lot about the other three hands. You know that opener's suit is likely longer than five, since both you and partner are short in it. Therefore, even if RHO turns out to have only two or three cards in that suit, they probably still have a pretty good fit. You also know that, even though they own the deal, their domineering power is only borderline. LHO and partner probably have each exactly 11 HCP. RHO probably has exactly 10. Thus, since they own the deal only by 21 to 19 HCP, and since they have already established their suit, you and partner must find your best fit as soon as possible if you want to remain meaningfully in the auction.

You and partner each have a three-suited hand. Moreover, you know that they are the same three suits. Are you going to just guess at a suit, thereby risking becoming declarer from the weak side in a Moysian fit? Or are you going to convey somehow to partner that you can ably support whatever his best suit is, and that he should make the choice so that the contract, if your side buys it, gets played from the strong side in a four-four or five-four fit? Obviously the latter, if you can.

Your bid of 1NT could not possibly be natural in this situation. Since your side has only 19 HCP together and since the opponents have a long, establishable suit to run against you, your 1NT could never be to play. Assign it then the significance of a responsive double, showing specifically 6-8 HCP, a singleton or void in the opponent's suit, and more or less equal support for partner in each of the other three suits. It must show 6-8, because with 0-5 you would pass and if you had 9+, then one or more of the other three players — probably opener — would be lying.

Klinger Doubles

Ron Klinger is one of the very best bridge authors to study carefully. Doing so will almost certainly improve your game. I long ago lost count of the many top boards I have achieved by playing his Rule of Ten and Twelve.

The premise of Klinger's Rule of Ten and Twelve is that penalty doubles of partial contracts are very lucrative if they can be done safely. The Rule of Ten and Twelve assures this safety. Klinger has figured out a two-part formula, an almost foolproof method, for deciding whether you should whack the opponents' part-score.[1]

It works like this: If you have determined that the HCP between the two sides split roughly 20-20,

[1] See Ron Klinger *100 Winning Bridge Tips for the Improving Player* (Boston: Houghton Mifflin, 1987), pp. 20, 22-23.

and if you are considering doubling the opponents' suit contract for penalty below game, you need two conditions to hold true:

First, count the trump tricks that just your own hand can reasonably expect to take, then add this number to the total number of tricks that the opponents are contracting to take. For example, say you hold KQxx in trumps behind opener and say that the opponents have bid to the 3-level. Add your expected one-and-a-half trump tricks to nine. That's ten-and-a-half. The first condition has been met. The sum is ten or more.

Second, count the trumps in your hand and add this number to the total number of tricks that the opponents are contracting to take. Continuing our example, add your four trumps to their expected nine tricks. That's thirteen. The second condition has been met. The sum is twelve or more.

Whack that contract!

Klinger's Rule of Ten and Twelve says: Double a part-score suit contract *only* if *both* (1) the sum of your expected trump tricks plus the opponents' total expected tricks is at least ten *and* (2) the sum of your trumps plus the opponents' total expected tricks is at least twelve. If neither or only one of these conditions is met, do not double.

Thanks, Ron!

Reopening Doubles

One of the most important aspects of balancing is the reopening double. Partners will love you for using this device — well, maybe not all the time, but at least 99% of it.

Say that you are in the pass-out seat holding a flat 8-HCP hand with no biddable suit and no stopper after LHO has opened 1 banana and both partner and RHO have passed. Partner is probably trap passing with pretty good bananas but no biddable suit, not enough HCP to bid NT, and the wrong shape for a takeout double. If she is not trap passing, then opener probably has a monster. It is now your duty to protect partner, to give her another call. With 0-7 HCP you would let the auction go. But with 8+ HCP, no stopper, and no biddable suit, you must reopen with a double. Do the math. It supports this action. RHO has 0-5 HCP. If he had more than that, he would not have passed as responder. That leaves 27 HCP to divide between LHO and partner. Even if LHO has as many as 15, leaving a minimum of 12 for partner, your side still probably owns the deal. You must therefore protect partner's opportunity to bid a contract, probably 1NT. Your reopening double gives partner the vital information that she needs. She can now add your advertised minimum of 8 HCP to her own HCP to learn which side owns the hand. She will then know what to do.

10

Responses to Partner's Overcall

I would be glad to receive some
instruction from my fellow partner.

— William Shakespeare
Measure for Measure, 4, ii, 15-17

Communicating clearly with partner so that you both
can exchange and evaluate vital information in a true
give-and-take relationship is always critically important, but even more so when the other side opens the
bidding. The side that opens has the advantage — at
least for the time being. The job of the overcalling or
balancing side is to take that advantage away, perhaps
even to turn it against the opening side. But such re-
versals of fortune require excellent teamwork between
overcaller and advancer. Stealing the opening side's
natural advantage is not simply a matter of overcaller
making the most obnoxious or obstructive bid that is
reasonably possible. This theft also depends on advancer knowing exactly what to do with that overcall —

and doing it in such a way that overcaller understands implicitly what advancer is up to. Is advancer adding to the obstruction or being constructive? Does our side want to end up declaring or defending this deal? Who is the captain? Systematic cooperation between partners is essential to answer such questions.

We already know that we expect our overcalls to be light and crazy. In keeping with our general strategy of aggression, we are not much concerned with suit quality when we overcall. We just want to get into the auction to disrupt the opponents' communication — and we will use almost any excuse to do it. Especially when we are non-vulnerable and they are vulnerable, an overcall of xxxxx, five little rags, is not unreasonable. More on that sort of thing later, in the section in Chapter 11 on "PLOBs."

But we also already know that advancer's duty is to rein in some of that craziness, so that the overcalling side does not get too high. The important point to remember, when advancing partner's overcall in this system, is that partner is quite likely to have terrible cards, an anemic suit, and a wimpy hand. If we forget this, we are going to get whacked for big penalties far too often. Aggression is fine, but foolhardiness is not. It pays to be careful, even when we are being a bit outrageous. If overcaller is wild, then advancer must be disciplined.

A plain vanilla non-jump overcall usually shows at least five cards and 7-15 HCP, i.e., a good 6 to a bad 16 HCP. We tend to discount the lower end of the HCP range, especially on the 1-level and even more especially when our suit is spades. Also, we may overcall a four-card suit[1] if we have decent length in the opened suit, a good suit to overcall, and a fairly strong hand,

---

[1] Following Mike Lawrence's recommendations for four-card overcalls in *The Complete Book on Overcalls in Contract Bridge* (Las Vegas: Max Hardy, 1979), pp. 6-10.

but for some reason cannot bid NT. Having established this pattern of cheap non-jump overcalls, partner then knows that whenever we make a jump overcall, we must have a *really* bad hand.

Advancer's single raise of overcaller's suit shows 6-8 HCP and at least three cards in the suit. A jump raise is preemptive, showing 0-5 HCP and at least four pieces. Likewise, a double jump raise is preemptive, showing 0-5 HCP and an even longer suit. Generally speaking, and especially when non-vulnerable, the weaker the hand and the longer the trump support, the higher the immediate jump raise should be. Remember the Principle of Fast Arrival. Trump length in this situation is advancer's most important consideration. With 0-5 HCP and three or fewer pieces, advancer should just pass.

Advancer's cue bid of the enemy suit shows at least 9-11 HCP and four pieces, i.e., a limit raise or better in partner's suit. Of course, if advancer is a passed hand, the cue bid is exactly a limit raise. If the opponents have already bid two suits by the time it is advancer's turn to bid, then, since advancer has the choice of which suit to cue bid, that bid can convey extra meaning. Cue bidding the lower of the two enemy suits shows the usual limit raise in overcaller's suit. If advancer is an unpassed hand, then cue bidding the higher enemy suit shows a game-forcing raise, i.e., 12+ HCP and four or more pieces in partner's suit; but if advancer is a passed hand, then cue bidding the higher shows 9-11 HCP and exactly three pieces. None of these cue bids tell or ask anything about stoppers in either of the opponents' suits.

Advancer's NT bid is natural and to play, based on the assumption that overcaller's bid is at the bottom of the HCP range. In other words, advancer should have at least 14 HCP and the enemy suit stopped to bid 1NT at least 16 HCP and a stopper to bid 2NT. Overcaller, at her second turn to bid, and assuming that advancer's NT is at the bottom of its range, may raise the NT strain, even to game, with the appropriate extra values. That is, overcaller should raise advancer's 1NT to game with 10+ HCP and advancer's 2NT to game with 8+ HCP.

Advancer's jump cue bid of the enemy suit shows a huge raise, forcing to game in overcaller's suit and showing interest in exploring for slam. Minimally, it guarantees first-round control of the enemy suit and excellent trump support.

With a powerful hand and exceptional controls, advancer may already be confident of the 5-level and may therefore jump right into Blackwood. With an incredibly shapely hand and fantastic controls, he may already be confident of the 6-level and accordingly may jump to 5NT as Grand Slam Force (GSF or "Josephine"), demanding that overcaller either bid the grand with two of the top three trump honors or sign off at the small slam with any other holding.[2]

Besides cue bidding, jump cue bidding, or bidding Blackwood or GSF straight out, there are two other ways for advancer to force overcaller to make a rebid: i.e., either (1) bidding a new suit at the cheapest level or (2) double jumping into a new suit.

Advancer's first obligation is to support partner's suit, if possible. We agree that advancer's new suit bid at the cheapest level is forcing only because it promises at least some support for overcaller's suit, in case overcaller cannot tolerate advancer's suit. With no support for overcaller's suit and no other reason to bid, you should not try to rescue partner by trying a new suit. Without support for her suit, just pass — unless you have a very strong hand and a self-sufficient suit of your own. What if partner has no more support for your

---

[2] The decision in this situation whether to jump to either Blackwood or Josephine illustrates once and for all the fact that shape and controls are more accurate, efficient, and important hand evaluators than HCP.

suit than you have for hers? Then there you are, a level higher and still in a misfit. Yucch! Your opponents are filled with glee, anticipating a big doubled set. Why? Just think about the likely distribution of all four hands. If you cannot support partner's suit and if she cannot support yours, then those cards still have to be somewhere, namely, in the opponents' hands, where they will not do you any good at all. So, even if you have a nice six-card suit to which you hope that partner could add two pieces, just pass the overcall unless you have at least two good or three not-so-good cards in partner's suit. Always, if you can, leave your side a refuge, a suit that you can escape back into if your prospecting for a better fit does not work out.

Advancer's double jump into new suit is a splinter, showing game-forcing values, a singleton or a void in that suit, control of the enemy suit, and three good or four not-so-good cards in overcaller's suit.

Advancer's jump into a new suit is preemptive. Not only is it non-forcing, but it also pretty much demands that overcaller pass rather than rebid. Advancer should make such a bid only if he has a weak hand and realistically believes that his suit is longer than overcaller's, i.e., probably at least seven cards.

In summary and for example, if LHO has opened 1♣, partner has overcalled 1♠, and RHO has passed:

If you hold:	Then your call is:
♠x ♥KQxxxx ♦Qxx ♣xxx	pass
♠xxx ♥KQxxxx ♦xx ♣xx	pass
♠xxx ♥KQxxx ♦Kxx ♣xx	2♠ (single raise)
♠xxxx ♥KQxxxx ♦xx ♣x	3♠ (preemptive)
♠xxxxxx ♥xxx ♦xxx ♣x	4♠ (preemptive)
♠xxx ♥KQxxxx ♦AQ ♣Qx	2♥ (forcing)
♠x ♥KQxxxxx ♦xx ♣xx	3♥ (preemptive)
♠Axxx ♥KQxxx ♦xx ♣xx	2♣ (limit or better)
♠Axxx ♥KQxxx ♦Ax ♣AK	3♣ (forcing raise)
♠Axxx ♥KQxxxx ♦— ♣AKx	4♦ (splinter)

♠xx ♥KQx ♦Qxxxx ♣AKx	1NT
♠xx ♥KQx ♦KJxxx ♣AKx	2NT
♠xx ♥KQx ♦AQxxx ♣AKx	3NT
♠xxxxx ♥AKQ ♦AQx ♣AK	4NT (Blackwood)
♠Kxxxxxx ♥AKQx ♦A ♣A	5NT (Josephine)

So much for responses to a simple overcall. But what should advancer do opposite a jump overcall?

Usually nothing, unless he can augment the pre-empt. Overcaller, after all, is expected to have a bad hand and a long, weak suit. The jump overcall, in keeping with the Principle of Fast Arrival, has probably already given advancer as much information as over-caller has to give. But, unlike in a simple overcall auc-tion, where the captaincy of the overcalling side is not able to be determined right away, in a jump overcall auction advancer is instantly recognized as captain. So, if he wants more information, he has the right and should have the means to demand it.

Advancer bidding a new suit forces overcaller to rebid, but again, advancer should never make this bid without a few cards in overcaller's suit. Additionally, at this elevated level advancer's own suit should be self-sufficient. Overcaller's rebid should support advancer's suit, if possible. Otherwise she should fall back on her own suit.

Cue bidding the enemy suit is also a way for ad-vancer to force overcaller. This is a more general force, asking overcaller just to rebid her suit with minimal values and a bad suit or to bid a feature with an honor or two in her suit and as little as Qxx outside. If part-ner's jump overcall was, say, 2♠, then the worst hand that advancer could have for this cue bid is something like ♠xx ♥AK ♦AQxxxx ♣AKx, in other words, within one trick of game and aiming for game in either NT or overcaller's suit.

11

Competitive Gadgets and Gizmos

This chapter offers some definite ideas and systems to interfere with your opponents' bids and systems in particular situations. The purpose of these interference tactics is to give your side the advantage in competitive auctions, no matter whether your side or theirs has opened the bidding.

Defense Against the Big Club

The fundamental structure of the Precision system revolves around an intermediate NT, 13-15 HCP, and an artificial 1♣ catch-all opening bid to announce nearly all hands of 16+ HCP. This bid is commonly called the "big club." Precision is one of many big club systems. It is probably the best.

There are oodles of ways to interfere with Precision. Nuisance overcalls are even more of a nuisance against Precision-playing pairs than against pairs who rely on a more natural system. Precision fares much better in uncontested auctions than in competitive ones. Precision openers especially hate to have their 1♣ bid overcalled. So make sure to overcall it at every reasonable opportunity!

Many of the popular direct seat defenses against the strong 1NT opening, such as Cappelletti, Brozel, DONT, etc., can be used (with the appropriate modifications) against the big club. For example, Cappelletti vs. the big club would look like this:

1♦ = hearts and spades, no worse than five-five. Advancer chooses.

1♥ = hearts and an undisclosed minor, no worse than five-five. Advancer passes or raises to choose hearts or bids an artificial 2NT as a relay to demand overcaller's minor.

1♠ = spades and an undisclosed minor, no worse than five-five. Advancer passes or raises to choose spades or bids an artificial 2NT as a relay to demand overcaller's minor.

1NT = unusual, takeout for the minors, no worse than five-five.

2♣ = undisclosed one-suited hand, suit no shorter than six. Advancer bids an artificial 2♦ to relay to overcaller's minor. Overcaller either passes or raises, with diamonds, or corrects to 3♣, with clubs.

2NT = unusual, takeout for the minors, no worse than six-six.

Double = penalty.

The Burger-Harrington (BH) defense against the big club[1] combines many of the better features of other

---

[1] Taught to me at the 1993 Albany Regional by my Swiss teammate Carl Burger, and devised by him and Paul Harrington.

defenses, such as Truscott, Mathé, Landy, Cappelletti, Brozel, etc. It gives the overcaller the ability to show all kinds of hands. Any bid on the 1-level shows the short suit of a three-suited hand (i.e., something like mini-Roman shape, although a five-card major is possible). Double shows shortness in clubs. The shortness should ideally be a singleton or void, but this is not a perfect world, and the need to interfere with the opponents' Precision system is so great that occasionally even a doubleton must suffice for shortness. On the 2-level, the BH defense is identical to the Cappelletti overcalls of 1NT. For the minors, BH uses 1NT to show five-five or six-five shape, and 2NT to show six-six or seven-six shape.

Defense Against the Weak No Trump

The best defense against the weak no trump may seem to be to double for penalty and watch the opponents run. That may net you 100, 200, 300, or even 500 sometimes, but it is a bad board for you if you have missed bidding a game by being so eager to penalize.

A better strategy is to use the methods described below, in the next section, for defense against the strong no trump.

Even better: Say that your partner in direct seat has just doubled an opening weak 1NT for penalty, showing powerful values. After responder has bid for a transfer escape, you recognize that with LHO's HCP values limited to 14, with partner's big hand, and with RHO's now-revealed shape and weakness, your side probably has a game or a partial in a suit that — so far

— only you know about. You have four choices, depending upon the strength of your hand and the quality of your suit:

First, with a one-suited hand, a weak or broken suit
of at least six cards, and little outside strength, you
can jump immediately to the highest playable level of
your partial. This is an instance of the Principle of
Fast Arrival. Partner, if he has extra values beyond
what he has already advertised with his double, may
raise you to game if he thinks it right. Example:

```
Dealer: N          ♠ K J x
Vul.: Neither      ♥ x x
                   ♦ K Q x x
                   ♣ K x x x

♠ x x x                          ♠ A Q T x
♥ Q J T x x x x      N           ♥ x x
♦ J T             W  ✧  E        ♦ A x
♣ x                 S            ♣ A Q J T x

                   ♠ x x x
                   ♥ A K
                   ♦ x x x x x
                   ♣ x x x
```

North	East	South	West (you)
1NT	Double	2♣ (transfer)	3♥ (to play)

Second, with a one-suited hand, a good quality suit of
at least six cards, and little outside strength, you
can jump immediately to game in that suit, depending upon your partner's hand for the necessary
strength in other suits. This is another instance of
the Principle of Fast Arrival. Partner may explore for
slam if he thinks it right. Example:

Dealer: N   ♠ K J x
Vul.: Neither   ♥ x x
                       ♦ K Q x x
                       ♣ K x x x

♠ —   ♠ A Q T x
♥ A K J T x x x   N   ♥ x x
♦ x x x x   W ◇ E   ♦ A x
♣ x x   S   ♣ A Q J T x

                       ♠ x x x x x x
                       ♥ Q x
                       ♦ J T x
                       ♣ x x

North	East	South	West (you)
1NT	Double	2♥ (transfer)	4♥ (to play)

Third, with a one-suited hand, a good quality suit of
at least six cards, and good outside strength, you
can force partner, if you are an unpassed hand, just
by bidding your suit at the cheapest level. A new suit
by an unpassed is always forcing. Example:

Dealer: N   ♠ K J x
Vul.: Neither   ♥ x x
                       ♦ K Q x x
                       ♣ K x x x

♠ x x x   ♠ A Q T x
♥ K Q J T x x x   N   ♥ A x
♦ J T   W ◇ E   ♦ A x
♣ A   S   ♣ Q J T x x

                       ♠ x x x
                       ♥ x x
                       ♦ x x x x x
                       ♣ x x x

North	East	South	West (you)
1NT	Double	2♣ (transfer)	2♥ (forcing)

Fourth, with a monster hand, perhaps with slam interest, you can force your partner by cue bidding the suit into which your RHO has just tried to transfer his partner. Example:

```
Dealer: N          ♠ K J x
Vul.: Neither      ♥ x x
                   ♦ K Q x x
                   ♣ K x x x

♠ —                           ♠ A Q T x
♥ A K Q J T x x     N         ♥ x x
♦ J T x x        W  ◇  E      ♦ A x
♣ x                 S         ♣ A Q J T x

                   ♠ x x x x x x
                   ♥ x x
                   ♦ x x
                   ♣ x x x
```

North	East	South	West (you)
1NT	Double	2♥ (transfer)	2♠ (cue bid)

Also, when your partner in direct seat doubles an opening weak or strong 1NT for penalty, and if opener's partner passes, then the full set of strong NT response systems are in effect. This makes sense because, after all, a direct seat double of any opening 1NT shows the equivalent of an opening strong 1NT or better. So, in that situation:

2♣ = Stayman.
2♦ = Jacoby transfer to hearts.
2♥ = Jacoby transfer to spades.
2♠ = minor suit Stayman, i.e., takeout for the minors.
2NT = invitational to 3NT
3♣ = drop dead, to play in clubs.
3♦ = drop dead, to play in diamonds.

3♥ = forcing to game in either hearts or NT.
3♠ = forcing to game in either spades or NT.
3NT = to play.
4♣ = Gerber.
4♦ = Texas transfer to hearts.
4♥ = Texas transfer to spades.

Defense Against the Strong No Trump

There are somewhere between a bazillion and a gazillion defenses against an opening bid of 1NT. They were mostly devised against the strong 1NT, but can usually be just as well or even better applied against the weak 1NT. Among the most popular in 2006 are DONT and Cappelletti.

DONT ("Disturb Opponents' No Trump") prescribes direct seat calls against 1NT as follows:

Double = any one-suited hand except spades. Advancer bids 2♣ as a relay to overcaller's suit. Overcaller either bids the suit or, if it is clubs, passes or raises.
2♣ = clubs and a higher ranking suit. If advancer cannot stand clubs, she bids 2♦ as a relay to overcaller's other suit. Overcaller either bids the suit or, if it is diamonds, passes or raises.
2♦ = diamonds and a major. If advancer cannot stand diamonds, she bids 2♥ as a relay to overcaller's other suit. Overcaller either bids the suit or, if it is hearts, passes or raises.
2♥ = hearts and spades.
2♠ = natural.

I don't like DONT because I want to keep that double in my arsenal available for penalty. The rule is very profitable that, whenever either our side or their side bids a natural NT, any subsequent double by our side is for penalty. I have gotten a lot of top boards that way.

An excellent way to utilize the penalty double of 1NT and at the same time enjoy ample versatility in multi-suited overcalls of 1NT is to play the Cappelletti system. In the ordinary version of Cappelletti (sometimes called "Hamilton"), an overcall of 2♣ indicates any one-suited hand, with that suit being at least six cards. Advancer bids 2♦ artificially as a relay to demand that overcaller either bid the suit or, if it is diamonds, pass or raise. If responder does not pass after the overcall, then advancer need not bid 2♦, since overcaller will get another chance to bid anyway. Instead, in that case, advancer may either pass or make a free call, typically either a natural suit or a penalty double of whatever responder has just bid.

We play a new version of Cappelletti, which is exactly like the ordinary version except that, if overcaller's six-card suit is clubs, then he just bids it immediately at the 3-level. This accomplishes two things: (1) It adds a preemptive aspect to the auction, thus giving responder a bigger problem, and (2) it avoids the useless relay sequence of 2♣ - 2♦ - 3♣.

So, the full schedule of new Cappelletti calls is:

2♣ = undisclosed six-card or longer suit, not clubs. Advancer bids 2♦ to require overcaller to name the suit. Overcaller passes or raises with diamonds, or corrects as necessary with a major.

2♦ = both majors, five-five or better. Advancer chooses one.

2♥ = hearts and an undisclosed minor, five-five or better. Advancer either passes or raises hearts, or, if he cannot stand hearts, bids 2NT to require overcaller to name the minor.

2♠ = spades and an undisclosed minor, five-five or better. Advancer either passes or raises spades, or, if he cannot stand spades, bids 2NT to require overcaller to name the minor.

2NT = both minors, five-five or better. Advancer chooses one.

3♣ = six or more clubs.

Double = penalty.

Cappelletti bids are all shape-showing bids, promising certain length in our suits, so we must be absolutely disciplined about this shape and length. Of all the things that you might lie to partner about, *do not lie to partner about length or shape!* Partner, especially if he is the captain of the auction, needs to have as precise as possible an estimate of the length of our best fit, in order to apply the Law of Total Tricks.

By partnership agreement, we play Cappelletti in the balance seat as well as the direct seat.

In addition to Cappelletti, Brozel at the 3-level works very well. Any overcall at the 3-level, except 3♣, shows a three-suited hand with a void in the bid suit. A three-suiter with a club void can be shown by bidding 4♣.

Defense Against the Gambling 3NT

The gambling 3NT opening shows a long running minor, usually no worse than AKQxxxx or AKJxxxxx, and no entry in another suit. There are two opportunities for defenders to interfere with the gambling 3NT: either in direct seat before responder has had the chance to either pass with both majors and one minor stopped or bid 4♣ as the signal to escape to opener's minor; or in the seat after responder has either passed or bid 4♣. In either of these seats, any 4-level bid of a major is to play. The major should be self-sufficient, i.e., at least seven cards or a very good six, and the hand should have significant values and controls in the other three suits, i.e., probably not less than 16 HCP. Starting at the 4-level is always dangerous. That's why people preempt.

Any 4-level bid of a minor is Ripstra. This shows the bidder's better minor as a takeout for the majors, whose shape is no worse than five-five. The demand for takeout is absolute unless the Ripstra bidder's partner has no more than two small cards in either major and has at least six good cards in the Ripstra bidder's minor. In that case, i.e., only if game in a major seems hopeless, either passing to convert or raising the minor to game is OK.

Ripstra is simple, effective, almost foolproof, but an occasion to use it has never arisen once in all the years that I have had it on my convention card.

A double of the gambling 3NT in direct seat is for penalty. A double by opener's RHO of responder's 4♣ escape relay is lead directing, promising high cards in clubs. A double by opener's RHO after two passes is Lightner-ish, asking opener's LHO to be extra thoughtful and creative about the opening lead.

A 4-level bid of either major in either direct or balance seat against the gambling NT is to play. Moreover, the overcaller or balancer fully expects to make this game. She should have a self-sufficient major of at least seven cards, sound controls in all three side suits, and no expectations of any tricks from partner. Examples of such a hand might be: ♠AKx ♥AKQxxxxx ♦— ♣xx or ♠AQJTxxxx ♥A ♦x ♣KQ. The partner of this major-suit game bidder should pull the bid only once in a blue moon — and even then only for incredibly extraordinary reasons. Here is an example of a deal where advancer would want to pull overcaller's game bid in a major:

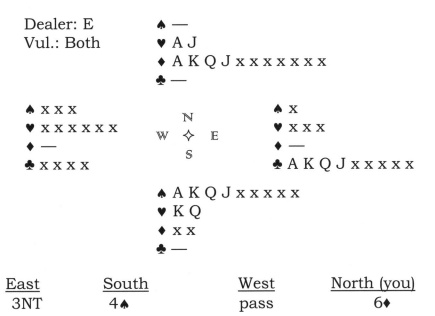

Dealer: E
Vul.: Both

♠ —
♥ A J
♦ A K Q J x x x x x x x
♣ —

♠ x x x
♥ x x x x x x
♦ —
♣ x x x x

        N
    W ✧ E
        S

♠ x
♥ x x x
♦ —
♣ A K Q J x x x x x

♠ A K Q J x x x x x
♥ K Q
♦ x x
♣ —

East	South	West	North (you)
3NT	4♠	pass	6♦

In fact, this contract makes 7♦, but there seems to be no way to determine whether declarer's ♥J is a loser.

Lebensohl vs. Weak Twos

Like all opening preempts, our opponents' weak two bids present several unique and difficult problems for us. That is why the opponents bid them. Specifically, how would we show the following hands after a weak two bid on our right? On our left? Long suit in a strong hand? Long suit in a weak hand? Flat 11½-14, 15-17, or 18-19 HCP with a stopper in the enemy suit? Flat 11½-14, 15-17, or 18-19 HCP without a stopper?

The Lebensohl principle has other applications beyond its original intention of effectively countering overcalls of your partner's 1NT opening. Chief among them is when LHO opens a weak two bid, partner doubles, and RHO passes, thereby showing both his inability to raise the preempt and his unwillingness, behind your partner's apparent three-suited takeout, either to redouble or to bid either a new suit or NT. In that case Lebensohl becomes very useful for your side.[2]

If you were just to bid a new suit, partner would not know whether to interpret your bid as drop dead or constructive. Lebensohl solves that problem. With a long suit and a good hand, just bid your suit. Partner will know that your takeout of his double is constructive. But with a long suit and a hand weak enough so that you want to sign off at the 3-level, bid 2NT as an artificial relay to 3♣. After partner obeys you by bidding 3♣, you can either pass if your suit is clubs or correct to your actual suit. Partner will know to drop dead.

That takes care of showing long suits after LHO's weak two, but what about some of those other hands?

Recalling the fundamental Lebensohl component that a Slow Approach Shows Stopper (SASS) while a Fast Approach Denies Stopper (FADS), you can, after partner's direct-seat double, cue bid the enemy suit to show the flat 11½-14 HCP, bid 3NT to show the flat 15-17 HCP, or jump cue bid the enemy suit to show the flat 18-19 HCP, all without a stopper. Alternately, if you have a stopper, insert the regular Lebensohl relay into the auction before you make these bids.

That takes care of all the hands we might want to show when LHO opens a weak two, but what about when RHO makes this bid?

With a long suit and a weak hand, just pass. *Don't preempt a preempt!* Have good values whenever

---

[2] The best discussion of this topic is in Ron Andersen's *The Lebensohl Convention Complete in Contract Bridge* (Louisville: Devyn, 1987), Part II, "Lebensohl After Opponents' Weak Two-Bids," pp. 57-76.

you overcall any kind of preempt. Wait for partner to reopen before you take action.

With a long suit and a strong hand, just bid your suit. With a long suit and an even better hand, double first, then rebid your suit. With a long suit and a gigantic hand, cue bid the enemy suit before rebidding your suit.

With a flat 11½-14 HCP hand, stopper or not, just double and wait to see what partner does. Also double with any flat 15+ HCP hand and no stopper.

With a flat 15-18 HCP hand and a stopper, overcall 2NT. With a flat 19-21 HCP hand and a stopper, overcall 3NT. Partner will escape to the 4-level if she cannot stand 3NT.

How to Cue Bid Properly

A cue bid in a competitive auction is any bid of a suit that the opponents have bid first, *if* their bid was natural.[3] If the opponents' bid of the suit was artificial and did not promise that suit, then our bid of that suit is natural, not a cue bid.

Cue bids are powerful indicators, versatile messengers, and effective communicators, always conveying artificial or conventional meanings, never natural. Also, if the opponents' bid of the suit was natural, then our subsequent bid of that suit can never be natural, even several rounds later in the auction. If we have their suit, then we either bid NT, trap pass, or double for penalty, but we do not bid it as if we wanted to play it ourselves. That would be dumb. Why would we want to declare against such an adverse trump split? Yet,

---

[3] There are also control-showing, slam-exploratory cue bids, but they are not our topic here.

strange as it may seem, there are some otherwise good
bridge players who believe that if they skip a round before bidding the enemy suit, then that shows a real
suit and should not be interpreted as a cue bid. Crazy
logic! What do such bidders think can be better accomplished by bidding the enemy suit naturally than by
trap passing, doubling for penalty, or bidding NT?[4]

Cue bids never show length in the enemy suit,
always shortness, often a void. As such, they tend to
imply length in at least two of the other suits. Many
treatments and conventions have arisen that are based
on this fact. Probably the most familiar of these two-
suited cue bid overcalls is the Michaels cue bid,[5]
which, if a minor, promises five-five in the majors and,
if a major, promises five in the other major and five in
an undisclosed minor. Partner is required to either
just choose a major or bid 2NT artificially to ask the
Michaels bidder to name the long minor. Michaels cue
bids are so valuable that, in our system, we play them
in balance seat as well as direct.

When playing Michaels — and indeed when playing any artificial two-suited overcall — you must be
rigorously, dependably, and unconditionally disciplined
about shape. Your suits must never be shorter than
five-five. That is because partner may have a doubleton in each of your implied suits, and will have to pick
one of the other. Do not risk dumping partner in a
four-two trump fit! Partner must be able to trust you
implicitly on the shape of your Michaels, Cappelletti,
unusual NT, and other obstructive, shape-showing bids.

---

[4] By the way, if you cannot bid NT for whatever reason, and if you are
therefore contemplating whether to trap pass or double for penalty,
consider whether the opponents have a safe place to run. It is better to
accept a sure one-trick set undoubled than to double the unmakeable
contract and in so doing scare them into running to a makeable contract.
The old shibboleth — *Don't double the only contract they can't make!*
— is quite valid.

[5] Named for Michael N. Michaels (1924-1966).

Most cue bids are made at the cheapest level, but a cue bid could also be a jump. What meaning shall we assign to this? Some pairs use it against an opening bid to show a strong one-suited hand. Others use it, also against an opening bid, to show the equivalent of a gambling 3NT opening hand, i.e., a hand with a long, strong suit and nothing else. Still others use it as if it were a splinter to advance partner's overcall, showing four-card support for partner's suit, a strong hand, and a singleton or void in the enemy suit. These are all good options, but these situations can all be handled well in other ways. For instance, in the last case, a splinter-equivalent is not necessary, since a non-jump cue bid shows a limit raise or better of partner's suit. Advancer will get another call.

Rather than any of these, we put the jump cue bid to another use. Have you ever been in second, third, or usually fourth seat, with a gargantuan hand, eagerly waiting to open a strong, artificial, and forcing 2♣, only to have RHO open in front of you? What can you do then? How can you show your monster now? A plain old cue bid would be Michaels. A double would not be strong enough. Overcalling would be really wimpy. Jump cue! This situation hardly ever comes up, but when it does, the jump cue bid is beautiful.

Above all, *never forget that all cue bids are forcing!* I will indeed never forget that, but I would like to forget the time I declared the enemy suit in a zero-three fit because my partner failed to recognize my cue bid as a cue bid — and passed.

Western Cue Bids

Say that partner has either opened the bidding or given some other clear indication of her strength, which, when you add it to yours, tells you that your side has enough power to play at some level of NT, usually 2NT or 3NT. Your side either has no fit or might have a minor suit fit. Of course you would rather play in NT than in the minor. You only need to know whether you can control the enemy suit.

The Western cue bid is a device that aims at getting a pair with sufficient combined HCP strength to play in NT if they can be assured of having a stopper in the advertised enemy suit. Usually in the second round of bidding, usually after your side has opened, and usually when you have not yet found a fit, a cue bid of the opponents' most recently bid suit asks for a full stopper in that suit, but promises nothing in the suit. The Western cue bid is typically, but not always, made by responder.

Some pairs play that a Western cue bid promises half a stopper in the suit and only asks partner for half a stopper to complement it. But what is the point of that? If you play that way, then you might as well go completely over to the other side and play Eastern cue bids, which show a full stopper rather than ask for one.[6]

Sometimes recognizing a Western cue bid is difficult. Difficult to recognize, perhaps, but not dangerous to fail to recognize it, since all cue bids are forcing. The cue bidder will get another chance to bid — and will then be able to shut the auction off in a suit if it seems obvious to him that partner has misunderstood the stopper-asking nature of the cue bid.

Here is an example of an auction in which you would naturally make a Western cue bid. Your side opens, has no apparent fit, but has enough HCP for game in NT. You only need to ask partner if she can stop spades. You obviously cannot. She can, but if she could not, she would run to either 4♣ or 4♥:

---

[6] William S. Root and Richard Pavlicek recommend Eastern cue bids in *Modern Bridge Conventions*, pp. 79-83, 226.

Dealer: N
Vul.: Both

♠ A x
♥ J x x
♦ x x
♣ A K T x x x

♠ J T x x x
♥ T x x
♦ K x x
♣ Q J

N
W ◇ E
S

♠ K Q x x x
♥ Q x x
♦ J T x
♣ x x

♠ x
♥ A K x x
♦ A Q x x x
♣ x x x

North	East	South (you)	West
1♣	1♠	double	2♠
2♣	pass	3♠	pass
3NT	pass	pass	pass

Even with just one spade stopper and an offside ♦K, 3NT still makes when the club honors fall.

Unusual Over Unusual and Other Invisible Cue Bids

The unusual NT overcall showing five-five in the two lower unbid suits has significant preemptive authority, but it does not pose an insurmountable problem for the opening side. Efficient methods are available for responder to show partner either the ability to compete or the willingness to penalize one or both of overcaller's implied suits.

"Unusual over unusual" is a species of "invisible

cue bids." The principle of invisible cue bids that, when the opponents make a two-suited overcall such as a Michaels cue bid or the unusual NT, both of these implied suits thereby become grounds for your cue bids, even though neither of them has yet been actually bid. For example, if partner opens 1♦ and your RHO overcalls 2NT, which artificially shows at least five clubs and at least five hearts, then both 3♣ and 3♥ become available to you as cue bids. Since you have a choice between two cue bids, you can — by prior partnership discussion — have agreed to convey different kinds of meanings with each. Thus invisible cue bids give you a wider latitude of what you can tell partner. An invisible cue bid made after an unusual NT overcall is "unusual over unusual."

Several ways exist to play unusual over unusual responses. Root and Pavlicek describe, but do not recommend, one of them in *Modern Bridge Conventions*, p. 242:

If partner has opened 1♥:

Your 3♣ shows a good spade suit and a strong hand.
Your 3♦ shows a limit raise or better in hearts.
Your 3♥ shows a preemptive heart raise.
Your 3♠ shows a spade suit and a mediocre hand.

If partner has opened 1♠:

Your 3♣ shows a good heart suit and a strong hand.
Your 3♦ shows a limit raise or better in spades.
Your 3♥ shows a heart suit and a mediocre hand.
Your 3♠ shows a preemptive spade raise.

This set of responses applies only to partner's major suit openings. But on pp. 83-87, Root and Pavlicek offer a more comprehensive system of invisible cue bids that applies to all conventional two-suited overcalls of partner's 1-level suit opening bid. Here is how the responses would look against the unusual NT:

If partner has opened 1♣:

Your 3♣ shows a club raise and about 6-9 HCP.
Your 3♦ shows a limit raise or better in clubs.
Your 3♥ shows a good spade suit and a strong hand.
Your 3♠ shows a spade suit and a mediocre hand.

If partner has opened 1♦:

Your 3♣ shows a limit raise or better in diamonds.
Your 3♦ shows a diamond raise and about 6-9 HCP.
Your 3♥ shows a good spade suit and a strong hand.
Your 3♠ shows a spade suit and a mediocre hand.

If partner has opened 1♥:

Your 3♣ shows a limit raise or better in hearts.
Your 3♦ shows a good spade suit and a strong hand.
Your 3♥ shows a heart raise and about 6-9 HCP.
Your 3♠ shows a spade suit and a mediocre hand.

If partner has opened 1♠:

Your 3♣ shows a limit raise or better in spades.
Your 3♦ shows a good heart suit and a strong hand.
Your 3♥ shows a heart suit and a mediocre hand.
Your 3♠ shows a spade raise and about 6-9 HCP.

In all of these cases a double is constructive, showing 10+ HCP, and a 4-level bid of any suit not implied by the opponents is preemptive.

Remember that in our system a minor suit opening could be the precursor to showing a 15-17 HCP or 18-19 HCP NT hand. That makes a difference. It makes opener's choice of rebids a bit more complicated. With either of these hands, stoppers in both implied enemy suits, and no apparent fit with responder, opener should usually just bid 3NT as a sign-off, but each situation will have its own unique features and should be played by ear. Depending on vulnerability, neither opener nor responder should overlook the possibility of a penalty double if the opportunity arises during the second round of bidding.

Another popular version of unusual over unusual is the following. In this version responder's double denies a fit with opener but shows the ability to penalize either NT or one or both of the opponents' suits.

If partner has opened 1♣:

Your 3♣ shows a preemptive raise in clubs.
Your 3♦ shows a limit raise in clubs.
Your 3♥ shows a forcing raise in clubs.
Your 3♠ shows a natural spade suit.

If partner has opened 1♦:

Your 3♣ shows a limit raise in diamonds.
Your 3♦ shows a preemptive raise in diamonds.
Your 3♥ shows a forcing raise in diamonds.
Your 3♠ shows a natural spade suit.

If partner has opened 1♥:

Your 3♣ shows a limit raise in hearts.
Your 3♦ shows a forcing raise in hearts.
Your 3♥ shows a preemptive raise in hearts.
Your 3♠ shows a natural spade suit.

If partner has opened 1♠:

Your 3♣ shows a limit raise in spades.
Your 3♦ shows a forcing raise in spades.
Your 3♥ shows a natural heart suit.
Your 3♠ shows a preemptive raise in spades.

The most important message in this section is that, if you want to use invisible cue bids, thoroughly discuss them with your partner first, to ensure that both of you understand the schedule and agree on the nuances of meaning.

Burger-Harrington Cue Bids

Say your LHO opens 1 kumquat, partner passes, and RHO responds 1 banana. If you have the other two suits and competitive values, you could double for takeout, or you could use the Burger-Harrington system of cue bids[7] to describe your hand even more precisely:

1NT shows five-five or six-five shape in the unbid suits.

2 kumquats shows six or more cards in the lower unbid suit and exactly four cards in the higher.

2 bananas shows six or more cards in the higher unbid suit and exactly four cards in the lower.

2NT shows six-six or seven-six shape in the unbid suits.

By implication, a plain takeout double in this position shows no better than five-four shape in the unbid suits.

PLOBs

A "PLOB" is a "Petty Little Odious Bid" or a "Petty Little Obnoxious Bid." Originally the acronym "PLOB" was applied only to a version of New Minor Forcing (NMF),[8]

---

[7] Again, taught to me at the 1993 Albany Regional by Carl Burger, and devised by him and Paul Harrington.

[8] NMF deserves to be insulted. It is far inferior to Checkback Stayman,

but now it applies equally to any gratuitous bid which is thrown into the auction for little other reason than to annoy the opponents. PLOBs may be either natural or artificial, but they are never psychic. Nowadays ethical bridge players do not psyche![9]

The best kind of PLOB is the crappy non-jump overcall in direct seat. To make such a bid you should have a quick trick or two and you must be within your partnership's agreed HCP range (say for example 7-15 HCP) on your convention card. Do not overcall — except to preempt — unless your hand is within this HCP range. Partner must be able to rely on your minimum point count in case she wants to bid NT. But, even though point count, quick tricks, and general hand strength remain important, in your present situation suit quality means almost nothing, especially when your side is non-vulnerable. Consider this deal:

```
Dealer: N        ♠ K 9 7
Vul.: N-S        ♥ A K J
                 ♦ Q J 6
                 ♣ T 9 8 6

♠ A T 8              N            ♠ 6 5 4 3 2
♥ 5 3 2                           ♥ 9 7 4
♦ A 7 2        W    ✧    E        ♦ 9 4 3
♣ 7 5 4 2            S            ♣ A K

                 ♠ Q J
                 ♥ Q T 8 6
                 ♦ K T 8 5
                 ♣ Q J 3
```

which accomplishes the same goal with less confusion. The PLOB in NMF is more of an annoyance to one's partner than to one's opponents.
[9] Nevertheless, a vast literature on psyches remains in print. The best book on the subject is probably *The Art of Psychic Bidding (and Its Pitfalls)* by Julian Pottage and Peter Burrows (London: B.T. Batsford, 2003).

North-South are playing Standard American with 15-17 HCP for their 1NT openers. Let the auction proceed: 1♣, 1♠, double, 2♠, then perplexity by North, who should be reluctant to bid 2NT without a clear fix on South's strength. With the negative double, South could have as few as 6 HCP. North would not relish playing 2NT opposite 6 HCP with the ♠A behind his ♠K. Of course, that fear is unfounded, but North does not know that.

What if North-South are playing our weak NT system? Would the PLOB bother them? Probably not. In the first place, if North opens 1NT, East no longer has the 1-level available and would be rather foolhardy to bid that suit at the 2-level. This is a clear advantage of AWNT over Standard American. After North opens 1♣ in Standard American, East is perfectly safe to overcall 1♠, even with that lousiest of all possible five-card suits. Even if West turns out to have a yarborough, East is unlikely to go down more than three at 1♠ with that hand. Even if doubled, down three is a bargain at 500 if North-South miss their vulnerable game. Without the PLOB, the auction is likely to go, with East-West passing throughout: 1♣, 2NT, 3NT. But with the PLOB interfering, North-South are less likely to discover their double stopper in spades and thus less likely to find their cold 3NT.

A PLOB does not have to be a low-level or first-round bid. Say that you are non-vulnerable against vulnerable opponents and your ultra-weak hand is six-six in hearts and clubs. RHO opens 1♦. Instead of immediately bidding your obvious overcall, the unusual NT, you pass and wait. This is a sort of trap pass. You know that you will get another chance to bid. LHO responds 1♠ and, after partner passes, RHO jumps to 4♠. *Now* you take action! Before LHO can initiate any exploration for slam with either control-showing cue bids or some form of Blackwood, you throw in a bid of 5NT! This can be nothing else than a takeout call for the two unbid suits. It preempts both Blackwood and cue bids. Your bid of 4NT would have accomplished the same takeout, but it would rob the opponents of only Blackwood, not cue bidding too. Over your 5NT, LHO could still bid 6♠ confidently with either a strong hand or sufficient controls, but your high-level PLOB may have kept them out of their best slam, perhaps a grand, which they would easily have found if you had either passed in the second round or bid the unusual NT in the first round.

I love PLOBs. I love to use them against opponents and I respect opponents who use them against me. Fortunately not very many of them do.

12

Bidding to Beat the Opponents' Slams

Lightner doubles are absolutely indispensable! Always discuss them with every new partner and make sure you both agree (1) to play them, and (2) how they should be played. Do not play with a partner who does not play Lightner doubles. They are indeed that important. If your partner is listening attentively to the whole auction, they are the single best weapon against otherwise unbeatable slams, for there is nothing declarer can do about the opening lead.

The principle of Lightner doubles is that to double a slam for penalty is at best useless and often counterproductive. This point is well documented throughout the literature of bridge. Thus the double of a slam by the defender not on lead is always to be interpreted as lead directing. It demands an unusual opening lead. Above all, if the doubler has previously bid a suit, it cries out, "Partner, whatever you do, don't you dare lead my suit!" If the doubler has not previously bid a suit, perhaps the double calls for dummy's first-bid suit. It always tells the leader to lead something weird, bizarre, unnatural. The whole purpose of the Lightner double is to call the leader's attention to the existence of an extraordinary state of affairs which the leader would be unlikely to discern on his own.

More often than not, against a suit contract, the Lightner doubler will have a void in a side suit. Thus the leader should not lead trump, but rather a suit in which there is reason to believe doubler may be short. Against a no trump contract, the Lightner doubler may have AQ behind dummy's KJ. Thus the leader should probably want to lead dummy's first-bid suit.

Another efficient but underused weapon against your opponents' slam bidding is the stripe-tailed ape double, so called because you must run like a stripe-tailed ape if they redouble.[1]

If you suspect that the opponents are bidding toward slam, you might want to double their game contract before they get a chance for control-showing cue bids or Blackwood. You do not expect to set this contract, but you hope that doubling it will scare them out of slam exploration. If it works, the mathematics is on your side. Bidding and making a small slam is worth 920, 980, or 990 non-vulnerable and 1370, 1430, or 1440 vulnerable. Bidding and making a doubled game with enough overtricks to make twelve tricks altogether is worth 650, 790, or 850 non-vulnerable and 950, 1190, or 1350 vulnerable. But the redoubled game with these same overtricks is worth 1000, 1280, or 1400 non-vulnerable and 1400, 1880, or 2200 vulnerable. That is why you must be ready to run like a stripe-tailed ape. If you make this double, be sure that you have a nice, long suit to escape into.

The best way to beat the opponents' slams is, of course, never to let them bid their slams in the first place. That is not often possible, but it is more frequently possible than many bridge players realize, especially at matchpoints.

---

[1] The irony being that apes do not have tails.

For example, say they are vulnerable and you are not, you are in third seat with a 2-count and partner is a passed hand. That gives your side a maximum of 12 HCP (or maybe a bad 13). Your opponents, therefore, are certainly destined for at least game and quite likely for slam. What can you do? *Get into the auction!* Overcall RHO's opening bid on *any* pretense — no lower than the 3-level and preferably at the 4-level or higher. The "sticks and wheels" (i.e., minus 1100) you are likely to suffer for a doubled five-trick set is a bargain compared to their 1430.

Still some respect for safety is warranted. You need some shape. Do not overcall RHO's opening, even in this situation, if you have a flat hand. But if you have a five-card suit, exploit it! If RHO opens 1♥, overcall 3♠ with ♠65432 ♥J96 ♦J43 ♣T5, or maybe even 4♠ with ♠QT986 ♥86532 ♦5 ♣76, but pass with ♠QT98 ♥865 ♦953 ♣843.

Here is a deal that was played in the Machlin Trophy Pairs at the 1995 Alexandria, Virginia, Regional:

Dealer: W   ♠ K 9 4 2
Vul.: N-S   ♥ 8 7 5 3
           ♦ A
           ♣ A K Q J

♠ A J 8 5   ♠ —
♥ J   N   ♥ Q T 6 4 2
♦ K Q 6 5 4   W   ✧   E   ♦ T 8 7
♣ 7 6 3   S   ♣ T 8 5 4 2

           ♠ Q T 7 6 3
           ♥ A K 9
           ♦ J 9 3 2
           ♣ 9

Sitting East, in third seat, white vs. red, with five cards
in their suit and a five-card suit of my own, I overcalled 3♥ after partner's pass[2] and RHO's 1♣. Look
how much bidding space they lost! LHO in fourth seat
certainly knew that his side would reap a big penalty
on defense at this point, but probably not as big as the
score they could get on offense, so he bid 3♠ rather
than double. They easily found their way to the right
contract, 4♠, but in many cases such obnoxious interference will make it difficult for the opponents to find
their right suit or their right level. What if, for instance, my partner had 5 HCP instead of 11 and LHO
had 16 instead of 10? Then my 3♥ overcall might have
proved very efficient in preventing either their getting
to the right slam or even their getting to slam at all.

However, a word of warning: Discuss this very
aggressive style thoroughly with your partner before
you sit down to play! I failed to do that on this occasion. Partner therefore naturally assumed that I had
something like a standard AQxxxx or KJxxxxx for my
preempt. On that basis, holding ♠AJ85 ♥J ♦KQ654
♣763, he doubled their 4♠, counting on me for some
defensive values. Disaster! Bottom board. His pass
would have meant an average result, i.e., no damage
done from my undisciplined jump overcall.

---

[2] I would have opened partner's hand.

13

Modified Roman Blackwood

Experts almost universally nowadays play some version of Roman Key Card Blackwood (RKC). That's fine. Let them. You can play it too if you want.

But you will never talk me into it. It is much too complicated a procedure just to take care of the trump king. One should never adopt a convention, especially a complicated convention, if one does not feel a need for it. I do not feel the need for it. I have seldom gotten into a bad slam where I wished I had known about the trump king so that I could have stayed out of it. The trump king may be more important than the other three kings, but not much more important. Not important enough to devote a whole convention to finding it.

More important to slam bidding than the location of the trump king is the question of the existence or non-existence of voids. Often the existence of a void in the Blackwood responder's hand is not revealed in the auction prior to the Blackwood query. If there is such a void, this is crucial information which the Blackwood responder ought neither to hide from the Blackwood bidder nor distort in any way.

Plain Old Blackwood (POB) is a great convention. But it is much abused.[1] Its purpose is not to get you into slams, but to keep you out of bad slams. Many pairs who ought to know better still use it as if it were a magic ticket into slams which really are not there to be bid. You should not use Blackwood unless you are prepared to go to the 6-level in your suit even if you discover that you and partner together have only three aces.

There are no "nevers" or "alwayses" among the tactical and strategic precepts of bridge, but one of the closest to an absolute "never" is: Never bid Blackwood if you have a void in your *own* hand! This simple admonition should be obvious — because in order to know whether to bid slam with a void in your hand, you must know exactly *which* aces partner has — but you would be amazed how many bridge players remain unaware of this simple principle. What if you bid Blackwood with a void in your hand and partner shows one ace? How would you know what to do? This slam will make:

♠ A   ♠
♥ —   ♥
♦ K   ♦ A
♣ K   ♣

But this slam will not:

♠ A   ♠
♥ —   ♥ A
♦ K   ♦
♣ K   ♣

Another "almost never" is: Never bid 4NT for Blackwood until the trump suit has been bid. The main rea-

---

[1] The section called "The Blackwood Convention," pp. 195-199, in William S. Root's *Commonsense Bidding* explains most of the dangers.

son for this rule is not to satisfy users of RKC or 1430 who need to establish the trump suit so that they can count the king of that suit as if it were an ace, but to prevent the Blackwood responder from misunderstanding the second round of the Blackwood part of the auction. For example, you open 2♣ with ♠AKQTxxx ♥AKQJ ♦x ♣x. You have a self-sufficient spade suit and need only one ace to make slam. If, after partner responds to 2♣, you leap immediately into Blackwood, and if you get the answer that you do not want, i.e., if partner shows no aces, then you are stuck. You want to shut the auction off at 5♠, but any new suit you bid at the 5-level is going to seem to partner like a relay to 5NT as the final contract, which in this case would probably be disastrous. The correct auction should include opener's spade bid in the second round, before Blackwood. Then opener can clearly and unambiguously shut the auction off at 5♠ after learning that partner has no first round controls in the minors.

Original Roman Blackwood (without key cards) works like this:

5♣ = zero or three aces.

5♦ = one or four aces.

5♥ = two matching aces, i.e., two major, two minor, two red, or two black.

5♠ = two unmatching aces, i.e., ♣A and ♥A or ♦A and ♠A. These pairs of aces are sometimes described as both round aces or both pointy aces.

Roman Blackwood is more informative than POB and not as troublesome as RKC or 1430, but, unless it adopts the special procedures that Root describes on pp. 197-198 of *Commonsense Bidding*, it cannot show voids. Furthermore, Root's methods cannot show all voids; i.e., Root can show only hands with a void and one or two aces, not hands with a void and no or three aces. But we can adjust these Roman responses specifically to show any pattern of aces and voids. Hence the Modified Roman Blackwood responses to 4NT are:

5♣ = zero or three aces, no voids.
5♦ = one or four aces, no voids.
5♥ = two aces, no voids.
5♠ = zero or three aces and a void.
5NT = two aces and a void.
Jump to 6 of a suit below the trump suit = one ace and a void in that suit.
Jump to 6 of the trump suit = one ace and a void in a higher suit.

The Blackwood bidder can then either decide the final contract or, if he wishes, ask for kings in the normal way of POB, with 6♣ showing none, 6♦ showing one, 6♥ two, and 6♠ three.

The only drawback to this version of Blackwood is that it cannot show a hand containing four aces and a void!

14

System Fixes

No bidding system is perfect. Sometimes a generally superior system yields an idiosyncratic bad result while a generally inferior system would yield a good result on the same board.

A "system fix" is a bad result that can be blamed on whatever bidding system a pair happens to be playing. That is, the bad result is not because of bad bidding, but in fact because of *good* bidding within a particular system. The implication is usually that, if a different bidding system had been in use for that deal, a better result could have been obtained — all other things being equal (which they seldom are).

One measure of the reliability of a bidding system might be the observed frequency of its system fixes relative to other systems. Precision has been touted as liable to fewer system fixes than so-called "natural" systems. K-S seems liable to fewer than Standard American. But — to the best of my knowledge — there is no hard data on any of this.

Standard American is easy to learn, easy to play, moderately accurate, and fairly safe from interference by the opponents, but it is not very tough on the opponents. Precision is difficult to learn, difficult to play, quite accurate, and quite tough on the opponents, but at the same time it is notably susceptible to any kind of overcall. K-S is a happy medium: harder to learn and play than Standard American, easier to learn and play than Precision; more accurate than Standard American, less accurate than Precision; almost as hard on the opponents as Precision, much harder on them than Standard American; slightly more susceptible to interference than Standard American, much less susceptible than Precision.

One example of a K-S system fix is this deal:

```
Dealer: N        ♠ A K 3
Vul.: Both       ♥ A Q 9 5
                 ♦ J T 6
                 ♣ K 4 3

♠ T 8 7 6              N          ♠ J 9 2
♥ K                              ♥ 8 7 6 2
♦ Q 8 4         W    ✧    E      ♦ A K 5 3
♣ A Q J T 7            S          ♣ 9 6

                 ♠ Q 5 4
                 ♥ J T 4 3
                 ♦ 9 7 2
                 ♣ 8 5 2
```

In Standard American, North naturally opens 1NT and it passes out. West would not be in much trouble backing into the auction with a 2♣ call in fourth seat, but still would be unlikely to bid, sitting underneath a big 15-17 HCP hand and not knowing how the spades and diamonds lie. 1NT makes easily. In fact, it makes two, with the defenders getting only four diamond tricks and the ♣A.

But playing a 12-14 or 11½-14 HCP 1NT system, North is obligated to open 1♣ or 1♦. South has no bid, and West is delighted to let it pass out. There is no way on this green earth that 1♣ or 1♦ will ever make. Yet North-South bid correctly.

Fortunately such fixes are rare in weak no trump systems. You can feel free to play the system without fear of your normal bidding methods sticking you with many bad results. More likely you will often find yourself glad to be playing the weak no trump on a certain deal because you will recognize that, if you had been playing Standard American instead, you would have suffered a system fix.

Besides ending up in the wrong strain, as shown above, another common type of K-S system fix is getting 3NT declared from the wrong side. This can easily happen when opener, with a flat 15-17 HCP, bids a minor and responder, with 6-9 HCP and no four-card major, bids 1NT.

Sometimes an attempt to escape from 1NT doubled results in a disastrous Moysian fit. For example, once in a club game this was the deal:

```
Dealer: N        ♠ 8 6 2
Vul.: E-W        ♥ Q J 9 5
                 ♦ A K Q 6
                 ♣ J 5

♠ A K 7                        ♠ Q 9 5
♥ A K 7 6          N           ♥ 8 3
♦ J 8         W   ✧   E        ♦ 7 4 3 2
♣ K 9 8 4         S            ♣ A Q 6 3

                 ♠ J T 4 3
                 ♥ T 4 2
                 ♦ T 9 5
                 ♣ T 7 2
```

North, Cameron Ross, opened 1NT. After two passes, West, Joe Fortino, doubled. Cameron passed, which, in the Baldwinsville Escape system, conventionally denied a five-card suit and demanded that South, I, start bidding four card suits up the line unless East, Bill Barrington, bid. Bill passed and I bid my only

four-card suit, spades. Joe doubled for penalty. Cameron, knowing that I had only one four-card suit, since I
had skipped all the others, had no choice except to
pass. So he played it in 2♠ doubled, down four, -800,
a cold bottom. If we had been playing Standard American, Cameron would have opened 1♦, Joe would have
found himself compelled to take action in the balance
seat, and we would have been safe. 1♦ doubled would
have gone down only one or two and our opponents
could have bid and made 3NT (which was the par
result on that board).

But for every system fix in K-S, there seem to be
many more system fixes in Standard American. A very
common type is when responder, sitting opposite a 15-
17 HCP NT hand, has a four-card major but is too
weak to bid regular Stayman and off-shape to bid Garbage Stayman. In K-S the 15-17 HCP hand is opened
1♣ or 1♦, and responder, with 6+ HCP, will bid her
major. The pair will find their eight-card fit, if it exists,
and will score 110 or 140. But in Standard American
the 15-17 HCP hand is opened 1NT, and responder,
with just 6-7 HCP, will pass. The pair will not find their
eight-card major fit and will score only 90 or 120.

Another common type of Standard American system fix vs. K-S is when the K-S 1NT opening prevents
the opponents from finding their low-level fit. Suit
openings at the 1-level are much easier than 1NT to
overcall effectively. Again the preemptive value of basic
K-S proves to be a winner!

15

Fifteen Pieces of Advice for Would-Be Experts

1. Read something — anything — about bridge every day!

Even if your reading is only five minutes spent daily with the bridge column in the newspaper, you must keep your mind actively engaged with bridge. Being up with bridge is just like the daily practicing that is necessary to master — and retain the mastery of — a musical instrument. Bridge is full of surprises. You never know what hand you will pick up. Who knows whether the problem you face this evening will be the very one that was solved in the paper this morning.

2. Pay more attention to your play of the hand than to your bidding!

Your long term results will be better with good play and bad bidding than with bad play and good bidding. The three best books in this area are: *The*

Play of the Hand at Bridge by Louis H. Watson, *Card Play Technique* by Nico Gardner and Victor Mollo, and *How to Play a Bridge Hand* by William S. Root. All three are indispensable.

Clyde Love's *Bridge Squeezes Complete* is fun, but can wait until you have mastered the techniques in Watson, Gardner/Mollo, and Root. Learn the basics that you will encounter every time you play before you try to learn the fancy stuff that you will encounter only once in a while.

3. Do not add any convention to your arsenal unless you feel a specific need for it!

Only add a convention if it takes the place of an otherwise idle or underused bid and if you fully understand all its implications for the rest of your system. You do not need a lot of flashy conventions to play any worthwhile system and you do not need all the conventions described in this book to play AWNT. In fact, most of them are unnecessary. The few essentials are listed on p. xiii and described in the appropriate parts of Chapters 2, 4, 5, 6, and 8. If you are uncomfortable with any particular convention — or if you are unsure about it — or even if you just don't like it — then don't use it. If you don't like it, then you probably don't need it — and if you feel that you don't need it, then you definitely don't need it. Keep things simple!

4. Play every board as if it were the match!

If you break concentration dwelling on how well or poorly you did on the previous board, you will almost surely get a bad result on the board you are playing now. Focus only on this one! Forget the last one. There will be plenty of time to rehash it later.

5. Take full advantage of every mistake the opponents make!

Be absolutely ruthless at the bridge table. Pleasant and courteous, a gracious and ethical competitor, but still absolutely ruthless. Cold, calculating, and always ready to pounce. No mercy! No prisoners!

6. Do not give up if you get bad results on early boards![1]

The first time I ever broke 70%, I got cold bottoms on two of the first three boards. But my partner and I huddled between the first two rounds, resolved to forget the first round, and never had another below-average result in that session.

7. Trust your partner!

When partner makes an apparently insane, treacherous, or subversive bid, give him the benefit of the doubt. To assume that partner is sane, on your side, and not subversive is a winning strategy in the long run. It saves the partnership when mistakes lead to bad results. Partner will sometimes make mistakes. So will you. Forgive partner's mistakes as he forgives yours.

When partner makes a penalty double that you do not agree with, do not pull it *unless* the auction has not yet revealed some relevant information about your hand which partner could not possibly have known earlier, and therefore could not possibly have considered while deliberating whether to double. For example, perhaps you psyched your opening, perhaps you have a void which would play well on offense, perhaps you have two extra cards in your agreed trump suit beyond what partner probably thinks you have.

Corollary to trusting your partner is knowing your partner. You must be aware of what each particular partner is likely to do in certain situations. Above all, you must know whether partner is a better or worse bridge player than you. Be honest about this! If partner is better than you, defer to him, try to make

---

[1] Unless we get cold bottoms on twenty-five of the first twenty-six.

him declarer. If partner is worse than you, mastermind the auction, hog the hand. Sizing up partner accurately will help you to develop the "table presence" that leads to good results.[2]

8. Ask yourself what partner did *not* bid!

Trying to figure out partner's bids is not always easy, but both of you will have more success and fun at the bridge table if, after partner makes a puzzling or even a seemingly crazy bid, you each assume during the auction that the other has made an intelligent call and that the hand may contain a problem which renders the right choice difficult.

When partner's bid confuses you, take a quick moment — in tempo — to envision the meanings of some of the common bids that partner could have made in that situation, but didn't. By picturing in your mind's eye some of the hands that partner could not hold, given the facts of the auction so far, you may, by process of elimination, create a less hazy picture of what partner actually does hold. After all, the whole purpose of bidding is for partner to give you as clear and distinct idea of his hand as possible.

9. Never lie to your partner — unless absolutely necessary!

Be aware that partner will neither know that you are lying nor, if your partnership is ethical, even suspect it.

Do not make off-shape takeout doubles. Do not shade NT ranges. Do not mislead partner about trump length. Do not promise a stopper that you do not have.

Sometimes lying to partner will be profitable, but try to keep it risk-free and rare. For example, when

---

[2] In *Bridge My Way* (Little Falls, New Jersey: Natco, 1994), pp. 51-60, Zia Mahmood tells some great stories about how to play well with an inferior partner.

partner is likely to become dummy, you might throw in a bid that misrepresents a suit holding or a control in order to misdirect LHO's opening lead, thus saving your side from first-trick harm.

10. Learn to love NT!

Some bridge players are "perpetual novices." They have reached a level of competence which is comfortable for them, and they have plenty of fun at the game, but they will never progress beyond that rather low level, no matter how many years or decades they play. They are known by three main traits:

1. They do not read bridge books.
2. They prefer club games to tournaments.
3. They do not enjoy being declarer at 1NT.

This third trait is the most significant, and marks a real line of separation between those who will never become experts and those who may become experts. All experts love to play 1NT! They love the thrilling challenge of manipulating card combinations in a roughly 20 vs. 20 HCP situation. It's the closest thing in bridge to a fair, bare-knuckles fight between declarer and defense.

If you use an AWNT system, you will play more than your share of 1NT contracts. You will also get more than your share of 90s, -50s, and -100s while pairs sitting in your direction at other tables are getting -110s and -140s because they allowed their opponents to start finding their fit at the 1-level.

11. At matchpoints, try to buy contracts in NT rather than in suits, if distribution allows!

With a 4-4 major fit and two flat hands, prefer NT. This is a decision for responder to make. With a four-card major but 4-3-3-3 distribution and game-going values, responder should decline to bid Stayman and should instead raise directly to 3NT. Declarer is likely to take the same tricks in either contract, and 630 or 430 looks much better than 620 or 420 at matchpoints. Such decisions are often risky, but risk is the name of the game at matchpoints.

12. Don't be a slave to your point count!

Terence Reese said it best: "... at no time feel that the number of points *dictates* the bid. ... the player who argues along the lines 'I had so-many points, so I had to bid such-and-such' is beyond hope."[3]

High card points really mean very little. They are just one tool among many for hand evaluation. Shape and controls are much more important. Open shapely hands lighter than their point count indicates.

Reese's advice is less important for NT hands. Since they are by definition flat — no singletons or voids, no more than one doubleton, no major longer than four cards, and no minor longer than five — their strength comes mainly from their high cards. So be strict about obeying the specified HCP ranges for opening NT. To put a good 14-HCP hand in the 15-17 NT range or a bad 15-HCP hand in the 11½-14 range is lying to partner. Sometimes your good hand plays poorly opposite partner's holding and sometimes your bad hand plays well. Partner needs to add your point count to his in order to determine the level of the contract. He's the captain. Give him an accurate number with which to do the math. Your NT bids should always show limits as trustworthy as the North Star.

13. Obey the Law of Total Tricks!

So much bridge is fought over the partial score, at matchpoints, at IMPs, and in rubbers alike, that any nuance of strategy which helps us toward accuracy in contested auctions must be a boon. Klinger

---

[3] Terence Reese, *Precision Bidding and Precision Play* (New York: Cornerstone Library, 1974, c1973), p. 3. Reese's italics.

doubles are one such tool. The Law of Total Tricks is another.

The Law of Total Tricks is a subtle, complex, variegated phenomenon whose story is told wisely and well by Larry Cohen in his two famous books, *To Bid or Not to Bid* and *Following the Law*. Absorb what you can. You don't need to understand it all. Even an elementary knowledge of the Law will improve your game. For example, just knowing not to bid eight over eight at the 3-level will garner quite a few excellent results.

14. Count! Count! Count!

Count everything. Count constantly. Count until it hurts. Count until you don't have to think about it anymore.

As soon as you pick up your hand start to count — and I don't mean just counting to make sure you have thirteen cards. Count your HCP. Then count everyone else's HCP. That's right. Even before the auction begins, count the probable HCP of the other three players at the table.

Count your longest suit. If it's a 7-bagger, figure that you and your partner probably have at least a 9-card fit (i.e., 13-7=6; 6÷3=2; 7+2=9), and should therefore finish the auction no lower than the 3-level unless you discover otherwise about partner's length. How quickly you get to the 3-level depends of course on your HCP strength. If you're in the opening seat with this hand, apply the Rule of 20 and open at the 3-level if your hand fails to meet the conditions of this rule.

Say you're in second seat with a 14-count. That means immediately that there are 26 HCP at the other three seats, or an average among them of 8 2/3 HCP. First seat bids 1 grapefruit. So now revise your count to give RHO a minimum of 11 HCP and a maximum of 19. That means immediately that there is a maximum of 15 HCP between LHO and partner, i.e., a maximum average for them of 7½ HCP. You pass. You have four grapefruits and no biddable suit. LHO also passes, and therefore is marked with a maximum of 5 HCP. This all means that RHO and LHO have maximums of 19 and 5 and minimums of 11 and 0 respectively, giving partner somewhere between 2 (i.e., 40-[14+19+5]) and 15 (i.e., 40-[14+11+0]). So partner most likely has around 8½ HCP, i.e., the average of 2 and 15, which would mean that you two together hold the balance of power. Partner had best reopen!

During the auction you can and should count the distribution of suits too. By the time the auction is over, you should have a fairly good numerical fix on the relative shape and power of the other three hands. When dummy hits, you can and should revise all your previous counting in light of this new information, whether you are declarer or defender. All totals are to be treated as working hypotheses, to be checked against each new bit of evidence that comes in.

Know where the power is; know where the length is; know where the shortness is. Keep track of it all. Remember it. For seven minutes. Then forget it.

Count! Count! Count!

You will never be a good bridge player if you don't.

But don't believe me about it. Go read the 25th day of Alfred Sheinwold's *Five Weeks to Winning Bridge*, the chapter entitled "How the Experts Count."

15. Lighten up!

Charles Goren said it best: "You should play bridge for fun. The instant you find yourself playing the game for any other reason, you should pack it up and go on to something else."[4]

---

[4] Quoted on the front cover of the ACBL *Bulletin*, v. 57, no. 6 (June 1991).

16

How to Overbid for Fun and Profit

A winning strategy is to overbid by one or two tricks, but only if you can successfully also overplay by one or two tricks.

In third seat, after two passes, you open 1♥ with ♠K94 ♥AQ542 ♦AKJ5 ♣5. LHO passes and partner responds 4♥, promising 0-9 HCP, five or more hearts, and a singleton or a void. You should immediately think about slam. 17 + 9 = only 26, but you have a great 17 and partner is unaware of your extra values. Do not pass. Use your imagination. You have a known fit of at least ten cards, first-round control of two suits, second-round control of another, and probable second-round control of the fourth. If partner does not already have ♥K, you are still quite likely to pick it up. All you need from partner to have a reasonable shot at slam is one ace. Any more than that is gravy.

This is one of many cases where Plain Old Blackwood (POB) shows its natural superiority over the various forms of Roman Key Card Blackwood (RKC). Playing POB, partner shows one ace and you confidently bid 6♥. But playing RKC or 1430, partner shows one key card. Is it an ace or just the ♥K? You do not know what to do. You cannot risk bidding 6♥ off two aces.

Fortunately there is another slam exploration technique that is safer, more informative, and therefore superior in general to all kinds of Blackwood. You can cue bid your controls up the line. So, after partner jumps to game, you bid 5♦, showing first-round control in diamonds and denying first-round control in spades and clubs. Partner, holding four small clubs and a stiff diamond, is not too excited to learn about your diamond control, but she can still bet that you have second-round control of spades and clubs, because, if you did not, you would not be exploring for slam in the first place. We could not blame partner for shutting off the auction at 5♥, because if she were to show her ♠A, that would commit the side to the 6-level. Nevertheless, she should trust you to have those second-round controls, in either high cards or shape, and imagine that her ♠A and ♥K, even though only 7 HCP, are going to be mighty important in the play of this hand.

Thus, by either POB or cue bidding, you land in 6♥ with a known total of no more than 26 HCP. No problem! As Marty Bergen would say, "Points schmoints!" Dummy comes down with ♠A762 ♥K863 ♦T ♣9632. You do not mind that partner lied about her trump length when she has both ♠A and ♥K. The only two things that could go wrong are a bad trump split and a failure to set up diamonds to pitch two losing spades from dummy. Above all you need trump to break two-two.

Opening lead is ♣A and you ruff a club at trick two. You pull trump in two rounds ending in dummy. Whew! Normally declarer does not finesse a singleton opposite an ace, but you have to do it now because that is the only way to make the contract. You run the ♦T and it holds. You ruff a club, pitch two spades under diamonds, and claim.

Trump splitting two-two is a 40.7% chance. The diamond finesse is 50%. So the 24-HCP slam is a

20.35% proposition. Those are not very good odds, even at matchpoints. But if partner had not lied about her trump length, you would have a ten-card fit where the odds of trump splitting two-one are 78%. The slam would then be 39%, which are not bad odds at matchpoints.

Take home message: If your partnership agrees on a general strategy of aggressive overbidding, be very reluctant to lie to partner during the auction.

But here's an exception. In bridge there are always exceptions. Say you are in fourth seat with a flat hand, 21 HCP, and an excellent four-card major. Normally you would open 2NT. Given the likely even distribution of the outstanding 19 HCP, you smell game. Even with as few as 4 HCP, partner is likely to raise your 2NT to game. The worst-case scenario is that partner has a yarborough, RHO has 9 not-very-important HCP, and LHO has 10 HCP and all the key cards to defeat you. But that is not very likely.

Say you get either a Stayman or a Jacoby transfer auction and end up in four of your major, which makes easily, maybe even with an overtrick. That result is all well and good, but it will not help you win any matchpoint events and it will be a push at IMPs. Same with 3NT. Flat board at matchpoints, push at IMPs. So let's try something a bit sneaky to get a superior result:

Open your convenient minor at the one-level, showing not your actual 20-21 HCP, but only 11+ ! A little white lie.

Partner is very unlikely to pass 1♣ or 1♦. If partner does pass, you are safe, because you would probably go down at 2NT anyway. But if partner bids, and whatever the opponents do, and especially if they bid, jump immediately to game. In that way you may induce them to double, which you can confidently redouble. A score of 880 or 1080 is better than 420 or 620, and a gain of 10 IMPs is better than a push.

The point is that you knew from the start that you could probably bid and make game in either your major or NT with that hand. The psychology of opponents is such that they almost never double a pair that opened 2NT, but they often double a pair that opened one of a minor. Give them the opportunity to make that fatal mistake.

Here's another deal: In first seat, vulnerable vs. not, you open 1♠ with ♠AQT53 ♥J642 ♦AQJ ♣4. After LHO passes, partner makes a weak jump shift to 3♦. RHO passes.

Now you reason that with unfavorable vulnerability partner must have a decent suit, probably at least seven cards headed by the king. She has no more than two spades and also rates to be shorter in hearts than in clubs. So you figure no diamond losers, second round control of clubs, a 50/50 chance to pick up all the spades on a finesse, and two or three heart losers. You bid 5♦, mainly on the power of your trump honors, hoping somehow to avoid disaster in hearts.

At this point partner can only figure you for excellent trump support and playable shape. She knows that you do not know about her ♣A. That extra trick is worth a stab at 6♦.

You are nervous about partner's raise to slam after her preemptive initial response, but even so, you are delighted when declarer's hand turns out to be ♠72 ♥3 ♦K975432 ♣A62. The spade hook works, trump split two-one, and the slam rolls home easily with only 21 HCP, but great shape and outstanding trump quality. It does not even matter what the opponents lead.

Annotated Bibliography

These are among the most useful books
for developing skills in duplicate bridge

American Contract Bridge League, *The Official Encyclopedia of Bridge* — 6th edition, edited by Henry G. Francis, Alan F. Truscott, and Dorthy A. Francis — (Memphis: ACBL, 2001). How can you live without this book? It has a little of everything, and a lot of some things: conventions, definitions, laws, histories, biographies, bibliographies, systems, stories, mathematical tables, suit combinations, etc., etc., etc.

Andersen, Ron, *The Lebensohl Convention Complete in Contract Bridge* (Louisville: Devyn, 1987). A thorough analysis and evaluation of a convention which is seldom needed, but very useful when it is needed.

Andersen, Ron, and Zenkel, Sabine, *Preempts from A to Z* (Stamford, Connecticut: Magnus Books, 1993). A magnificent book on modern methods of aggressive but disciplined interference in the opponents' auctions, describing and analyzing many specific conventions, treatments, strategies, and decisions, as well as offering abundant nuggets of wisdom on bidding in general.

Bergen, Marty, *Better Bidding With Bergen, Volume One: Uncontested Auctions* (Las Vegas: Max Hardy, 1985). The *locus classicus* of such key concepts in modern aggressive bidding methods as: "Bergen raises" (pp. 37-43), allowing easier and more consistent compliance with the Law of Total Tricks; skipping long diamonds after partner opens 1♣ in order to respond in a four-card major immediately; opening high-level preempts; etc. You don't have to agree with everything Bergen says, but you should know it anyway, because you are going to encounter a lot of opponents — including me! — who use his methods.

Bergen, Marty, *Better Bidding With Bergen, Volume Two: Competitive Bidding, Fit Bids, and More* (Las Vegas: Max Hardy, 1986). This book should be subtitled, *How to Distort Your Opponents' Auctions.* Bergen got where he is by doing just that. Absorb Bergen's principles contained herein, as well as in *Points Schmoints!* and in his regular column in the ACBL *Bulletin,* and you will find that not only have you generated more confusion for your opponents, and made it more difficult for them to discover their best contract, but also improved the accuracy and timeliness of communication with your own partner, and made it easier to discover whether it is best for you to play or defend, at what level, and in what strain.

Bergen, Marty, *Everyone's Guide to the New Convention Card* (Little Falls, New Jersey: Natco, 1994). More than just a crutch for the bewildered in the face of ever more complex ACBL rules and regulations, it also offers interpretation and rationale of the various conventions and treatments listed on the convention card, as well as a glossary and concordance to *Better Bidding with Bergen.*

Bergen, Marty, *Points Schmoints! Bergen's Winning Bridge Secrets* (Stamford, Connecticut: Magnus, 1995). Further distillation and clarification of the basic principles set forth in *Better Bidding With Bergen,* but aimed at a more general audience. Outrageous! You'll love his stories.

Bridge: Classic and Modern Conventions, 4 volumes, edited by Magnus Lindkvist (Bucharest: Arta Grafica, 2001-2003). Monumental, ambitious, and encyclopedic, but uneven. A noble effort to capture what probably never can be captured: the full spectrum of bridge conventions in common use throughout the world.

Cohen, Larry, *Following the Law: The Total Tricks Sequel* (Little Falls, New Jersey: Natco, 1994). Stories, illustrations, exceptions, refinements, objections, answers to objections, etc., all directed toward further elucidation of the LAW — (yes, following Cohen's own practice, the word is often written in all caps when it refers to "The Law of Total Tricks").

Cohen, Larry, *To Bid or Not to Bid: The Law of Total Tricks* (Little Falls, New Jersey: Natco, 1992). The most important book on a single principle of bidding. Few can expect to win consistently nowadays who have not made obeying the LAW second nature. Nevertheless, some experts object; cf. Mike Lawrence's and Anders Wirgren's *I Fought the Law of Total Tricks*, below.

Feldheim, Harold, *Five Card Major Bidding in Contract Bridge* (Port Chester, New York: Barclay Bridge Supplies, 1985). A clear and neat explication of most aspects of a treatment which has become a basic premise of bridge in the wake of Goren, Kaplan-Sheinwold, and Precision.

Feldheim, Harold, *Winning Swiss Team Tactics* — new and revised — (Branford, Connecticut: Lorold Associates, 1993). A complete guide to bidding and play at IMPs.

Granovetter, Pamela and Matthew, *A Switch in Time* (Cleveland: Granovetter Books, 1994). A perceptive analysis of common problems on defense and practical suggestions for solving them.

Grant, Audrey, and Rodwell, Eric, *Bridge Maxims: Secrets of Better Play* (New York: Prentice-Hall, 1987). Even though this entertaining text is aimed at beginners, it contains a lot of advice on the play of the hand that even experts would do well not to forget.

Hall, Burt, and Rose-Hall, Lynn, *How the Experts Win at Bridge* (Lake Worth, Florida: Jordan, 1996). A splendid all-purpose guide to fine-tuning your game.

Hamman, Bob, with Manley, Brent, *At the Table: My Life and Times* (Memphis: DBM Publications, 1994). The bridge autobiography of one of the best players of all time, giving the rest of us a view of how winners think.

Jacoby, James, *Jacoby on Bridge* (New York: Pharos, 1987). A short but thorough book on the fundamentals of Oswald Jacoby's winning style of bridge.

Kantar, Edwin B., *Defensive Bridge Play Complete* (North Hollywood, California: Wilshire Book Company, 1974). Familiarly and affectionately known as "The Big Red Book," absolutely indispensable toward mastering the aspect of the game that really separates the winners from the also-rans: defense.

Kaplan, Edgar, *Bridge Master: The Best of Edgar Kaplan* (New York: Bridge World Books, 2004). A selection of Kaplan's columns from the *Bridge World*, the premier periodical in the field, which he edited for thirty years.

Kaplan, Edgar, "Kaplan-Sheinwold Updated" (Chicago: Nella Bridge Supplies, [n.d.]), reprint of an article that originally appeared in the *Bridge World*. A bare-bones outline of a version of the K-S system (or, as Kaplan says, "collection of sub-systems") developed after the two editions of *How to Play Winning Bridge*. This summary is also online at the Bridge World magazine Web site: <www.bridgeworld.com/default.asp?d=editorial_dept&f=edgarkaplan/ksupdated.html>.

Kaplan, Edgar, and Sheinwold, Alfred, *How to Play Winning Bridge* — 1st edition — (New York: Fleet, 1958). This book revolutionized bridge by introducing the weak no trump system that soon became known as "Kaplan-Sheinwold." Now long out of print and hard to locate, but it is well worth the search if you can find it.

Kaplan, Edgar, and Sheinwold, Alfred, *How to Play Winning Bridge* — 2nd edition — (New York: Collier, 1962). A slight revision of their 1958 classic.

Kearse, Amalya, *Bridge Conventions Complete* — revised and expanded — (Louisville: Devyn, 1990). Not quite "complete," but wide-ranging. Indeed it would be impossible to make a "complete" list of bridge conventions, even just the good ones, since there are so many of them, and many more all the time. Nevertheless, there are many significant omissions, e.g., the jump cue bid to show a strong one-suited hand, as described on p. 166 of Root and Pavlicek, the Eastern cue bid, as described on p. 79 of Root and Pavlicek, the ACOL 3NT opening, as described on p. 107 of Root and Pavlicek, and quite a few specialized bids associated with weak no trump systems, Precision, etc. More comprehensive and more up-to-date, but not necessarily better, is *Bridge: Classic and Modern Conventions*, edited by Magnus Lindkvist.

Kelsey, Hugh, *Simple Squeezes* (Boston: Houghton Mifflin, 1995). Next to Clyde Love, the second best book on a very important aspect of declarer play.

Kelsey, Hugh, *The Tricky Game: Deceptive Plays to Win-*

ning Bridge (Louisville: Devyn, 1982). Expert instruction on how to confuse the opponents with sneaky card play on both offense and defense.

Kleinman, Danny, *The No Trump Zone* (Toronto: Master Point Press, 2004). A full and cogent exploration of the intricacies of NT bidding, including analysis of the justifications for the various opening NT ranges.

Klinger, Ron, *Bid Better, Much Better, After Opening 1 No-Trump: Bidding to Win at Bridge* (London: Cassell, 2001). Some radical but reasonable suggestions.

Klinger, Ron, *Guide to Better Duplicate Bridge* — Standard American edition — (Boston: Houghton Mifflin, 1996). A step-by-step guide to specialized bidding, aimed primarily at intermediate players, with plenty of exercises, problems, and quizzes. Klinger's Chapters 14 and 15 on cue bids are especially worth several careful readings.

Klinger, Ron, and Kambites, Andrew, *How Good is Your Bridge Hand* (London: Victor Gollancz, 2000). Clues to evaluation and reevaluation at various stages of the auction and appropriate bidding to reflect those judgments.

Klinger, Ron, *Improve Your Bridge Memory* (London: Victor Gollancz, 1984). Hints and exercises designed to cover specific situations and to teach you how to ease the strain on your memory so that your mind will be free to concentrate more intensely on analysis and judgment at the table.

Klinger, Ron, *100 Winning Bridge Tips for the Improving Player* (Boston: Houghton Mifflin, 1987). Any bridge book by Ron Klinger is well worth reading, but this one even more so for just one reason: "The Klinger Double," described in Tips 10 and 12.

Lawrence, Mike, *The Complete Book on Balancing in Contract Bridge* (Las Vegas: Max Hardy, 1981). Keen analysis of the various kinds of situations which require a balancing bid. Lawrence emphasizes how important it is for partners to discuss such contingencies in detail *before* they arrive at the table.

Lawrence, Mike, *The Complete Book on Overcalls in Contract Bridge* (Las Vegas: Max Hardy, 1979). Like all of Lawrence's books, this one is loaded with pearls of wisdom, such as the idea (explained in his Chapter Two) that overcalling a good four-card suit in second seat is OK if you have length in RHO's suit, because that distribution increases the probability that partner will have a fit with your suit.

Lawrence, Mike, *How to Read Your Opponents' Cards: The Bridge Experts' Way to Locate Missing High Cards* — 2nd edition — (Louisville: Devyn, 1986). Without peeking, of course.

Lawrence, Mike, and Wirgren, Anders, *I Fought the Law of Total Tricks* (Brentwood, Tennessee: Mikeworks, 2004). Well reasoned criticism of the LAW, may cause Larry Cohen to lose some sleep. Also contains a reprint of Jean-René Vernes original 1969 article, "The Law of Total Tricks," from the *Bridge World*.

Lawrence, Mike, *Opening Leads* (Los Alamitos, California: C & T Bridge Supplies, 1996). Intends to take some of the guesswork out of the most mysterious — and yet probably the most consequential — aspect of defense.

Lawrence, Mike, and Hanson, Keith, *Winning Bridge Intangibles* (Louisville: Devyn, 1985). Just a tiny pamphlet, but power-packed with reliable advice for maintaining composure, cleverness, and concentration at the table, in order best to soothe partner and smash the opponents.

Love, Clyde E., *Bridge Squeezes Complete, or: Winning End Play Strategy* (New York: Dover, 1968). The best book on a very important aspect of declarer play.

McMullin, Edith Titterton, *Adventures in Duplicate Bridge* — revised edition — (Memphis: ACBL, 1989). A fundamental, general, and humorous manual for novices at duplicate (with Jude Goodwin's charming illustrations and plenty of McMullin's legendary anecdotes), emphasizing differences between duplicate and rubber bridge, introducing moderately aggressive bidding methods in short chapters such as "Bids Your Mother Never Taught You," and wisely urging not adopting bidding conventions unless you "feel pain" from not having them in your arsenal.

Meckstroth, Jeff, *Win the Bermuda Bowl With Me* (Toronto: Master Point Press, 2001). Entertaining, authoritative, and educational. What more could you want?

Mollo, Victor, and Gardner, Nico, *Card Play Technique, or:*

The Art of Being Lucky (London: Faber and Faber, 1971). Next to Watson, the second best book on declarer play. (Sometimes Gardner is listed as the first author.)

Reese, Terence, *Precision Bidding and Precision Play* (New York: Cornerstone Library, 1974, c1973). This is an effective outline of the Precision bidding system; but even more valuable, and of general application to *all* bridge players, Precision bidders or not, is the following insight, which cannot be overstated: "... the player who argues along the lines 'I had so-many points, so I had to bid such-and-such' is beyond hope" (p. 3). Marty Bergen later developed such disregard for high card points into a fine art.

Reese, Terence, and Bird, David, *All You Need to Know About Play* (Boston: Houghton Mifflin, 1995). This book is not titled accurately — in fact it contains only a little of what declarers and defenders need to know — but its few tidbits of knowledge are essential.

Rigal, Barry, *Step-by-Step Deception in Defence* (London: B.T. Batsford, 1997). A book of problems and examples which, if studied carefully in conjunction with Kelsey's *Tricky Game* and any good defensive manual such as Kantar's "Red Book," Root's *How to Defend*, or Sydnor's *How to Set Your Opponents*, could dramatically enhance your defensive skills.

Root, William S., *Commonsense Bidding* (New York: Crown, 1986). Shorter and easier to read than Goren, this book is a great argument-settler. It gives the definitive outline of modern Standard American bidding, i.e., not the wild, crazy, and ultra-complicated bidding systems that experts play, but the ordinary simple methods that rubber bridge players and new — or relatively new — duplicate players prefer. For example, the opening no trump ranges here are 16-18, 21-23, and 24-26, not the 15-17, 20-21, and gambling 3NT that experienced tournament players now favor. The world would be a better place if every bridge player were to study Root's section on Blackwood (pp. 195-199).

Root, William S., *How to Defend a Bridge Hand* (New York: Crown, 1994). Accessible, clearly written examples, analysis, problems, and quizzes for novices and intermediates.

Root, William S., *How to Play a Bridge Hand* (New York: Crown, 1990). Next to Watson and Mollo/Gardner, the third best book on declarer play.

Root, William S., and Pavlicek, Richard, *Modern Bridge Conventions* (New York: Crown, 1981). Words cannot express the tremendous benefit this book has been to my bridge game! It is a bit out-of-date now, as many useful and popular conventions — e.g., Cappelletti (a.k.a. Hamilton) and D.O.N.T. — have appeared since 1981, but Root's and Pavlicek's analyses of basic bidding situations will remain cogent forever. They are particularly insightful on which bidding conventions are compatible or incompatible with which others.

Sheinwold, Alfred, *5 Weeks to Winning Bridge* (New York: Trident, 1964). It's true! Read one chapter of this book each day for 35 days, and at the end of that time you will be a better bridge player. Especially important is the 25th day: "How the Experts Count."

Simon, S.J., *Why You Lose at Bridge* (New York: Simon and Schuster, 1946). Classic insight into the psychology of the game — funny too! This is the first bridge book I ever read. It was one of my dad's favorites. He recommended it to me when I was a teenager, and I think this is what hooked me on bridge for life.

Stewart, Frank, *Better Bridge for the Advancing Player: An Introduction to Constructive Thinking at the Bridge Table* (Englewood Cliffs, New Jersey: Prentice-Hall, 1984). An eclectic, amusing, and enlightening collection of "story problems."

Stewart, Frank, *The Bridge Player's Comprehensive Guide to Defense* (New York: Dodd, Mead, 1988). A thorough and insightful treatise on all aspects of bridge defense for all levels of players, with quizzes, examples, detailed analyses, and even a "final exam."

Stewart, Frank, *Winning Defense for the Advancing Bridge Player: More Constructive Thinking at the Bridge Table* (Englewood Cliffs, New Jersey: Prentice-Hall, 1985). Plenty of practical exercises to improve the logical process of making fast and accurate defensive decisions.

Sydnor, Caroline, *Bridge Made Easy, Book Four: How to Set Your Opponents* (Alexandria, Virginia: Caroline Sydnor, 1992). A basic outline of defensive techniques for novices and intermediates.

Teukolsky, Roselyn, *How to Play Bridge With Your Spouse ... and Survive!* (Toronto: Master Point Press, 2002). Fun stories that offer heartfelt insight into the proper care and feeding of partners.

Truscott, Alan, *Doubles and Redoubles* (New York: Times Books, 1987). The title of this stellar selection of Truscott's *New York Times* columns is misleading, since much more than just the topic of whacking and rewhacking is covered. Truscott is always entertaining and instructive.

Truscott, Alan, and Alder, Philip, *On Bidding: Albert Morehead's Classic Work on the Principles of Bidding Judgment* (New York: Fireside, 1990). Clear historical and conceptual exposition of bidding theory. The fundamental principles expressed in this book are applicable to any bidding system.

Truscott, Dorothy Hayden, *Winning Declarer Play* (North Hollywood, California: Wilshire Book Company, 1969). The fourth best book on declarer play, after Watson, Mollo/Gardner, and Root.

Watson, Louis H., *Watson's Classic Book on the Play of the Hand at Bridge* — new edition, enlarged and modernized by Sam Fry, Jr. — (New York: Barnes & Noble, 1958). Even though the first edition appeared in 1934 when contract bridge was in its childhood, this text has never been surpassed. It is simply the best book on declarer play ever, with quite a bit of valuable insight into defense as well.

Woolsey, Kit, *Matchpoints* (Louisville: Devyn, 1982). An expert dissertation on the particular type of bidding needed to win at matchpoints.

Zia Mahmood, *Bridge My Way* (Little Falls, New Jersey: Natco, 1994). Charismatic and provocative, the ultimate autobiographical look at bridge intangibles, especially the most elusive advantage: "table presence."

SPECIAL DOUBLES

After Overcall: Penalty ☐ _____
Negative ☒ thru _3♠_____
Responsive ☒ thru _3♠___ Maximal ☐
Support Dbl ☐ thru _____ Redbl ☐
Card-showing ☐   Min. Offshape T/O ☐

NOTRUMP OVERCALLS

Direct: _15_ to _18_ Systems On ☒
Conv. ☐ _____ systems for strong NT
Balancing: _____11_____ to _____14_____
Jump to 2NT: Minors ☐ 2 Lowest ☒
Conv. ☐ _____ at least 5-5

SIMPLE OVERCALL

1 level _7_ to _15_ HCP (usually)
often 4 cards ☐   very light style ☒

Responses

New Suit: Forcing ☒ NF Const ☐ NF ☐
Jump Raise: Forcing ☐ Inv. ☐ Weak ☒
cue bid = limit raise or better

DEFENSE VS NOTRUMP

vs. _weak or strong_ _____
2♣ _one suit (6+) not clubs_
2♦ _majors (5-5 or better)_
2♥ _hearts (5+) & minor (5+)_
2♠ _spades (5+) & minor (5+)_
Dbl _penalty_   _penalty_
Other _2NT = minors (5-5 or better)_
3♣ = clubs (6+)

JUMP OVERCALL

Strong ☐   Intermediate ☐   Weak ☒
_____ could be very weak non-vul

OVER OPP'S T/O DOUBLE

New Suit Forcing: 1 level ☒ 2 level ☐
Jump Shift: Forcing ☐ Inv. ☐ Weak ☒
Redouble Implies ~~no fit~~ ☒ 10+ HCP

2NT Over	Limit	Limit	Weak
Majors	☐	☐	☐
Minors	☐	☐	☐
Other	_____		

OPENING PREEMPTS

	Sound	Light	Very Light
3/4-bids	☐	☒ vul	☒ non-vul

Conv./Resp. _____Namyats_____

Balance or **DIRECT CUEBID**

OVER:	Minor	Major	Artif. Bids
Natural	☐	☐	☐
Strong T/0	☐	☐	☐
Michaels	☒	☒	☐

Jump cue = monster 1-suiter, equivalent
of 2♣ opener; Michaels = at least 5-5

VS Opening Preempts Double Is

Takeout ☒ thru _3♠_____ Penalty ☐
Conv. Takeout _____
Lebensohl 2NT Response ☒
Other: _____
_____

SLAM CONVENTIONS   Gerber ☒: 4NT: Blackwood ☒ RKC ☐ 1430 ☐

Gerber = only direct jump over 1NT or 2NT opener or over sequences showing 15-17,
18-19, 22-23 HCP flat; 4NT quantitative only when Gerber available, o/w B-wood.
Modified Roman Blackwood: 5♣ = 0-3 aces w/o void, 5♦ = 1-4 aces w/o void, 5♥ = 2 aces
w/o void, 5♠ = 0-3 aces w/ void, 5NT = 2 aces w/ void, jump to 6-level below trump suit = 1
ace w/ void in that suit, jump to 6 of trump suit = 1 ace w/ void in higher ranking suit.
vs. Interference: DOPI ☒   DEPO ☒   Level: _____ ROPI ☐

LEADS (Circle card led, if not in bold)

versus Suits		versus Notrump	
(x)x	(x)xxx	(x)x	(x)xxx
(x)xx	(x)xxxx	(x)xx	(x)xxxx
AKx	T9x	AKJx	AQJx
KQx	KJ(T)x	AJ(T)9	AT9x
QJx	KT9x	**KQJx**	KQT9
JTx	QT9x	**QJTx**	QT9x
KQT9		JT9x	T9xx

LENGTH LEADS:

4th Best	vs SUITS ☒	vs NT ☒
3rd/5th Best	vs SUITS ☐	vs NT ☐
	Attitude vs NT ☐	

J denies, ten implies; 4th best promises honor
Primary signal to partner's leads
Attitude ☒   Count ☐   Suit Preference ☐

DEFENSIVE CARDING

	vs SUITS	vs NT
Standard:	☒	☒
Except ☐		
Upside-Down		
count	☐	☐
attitude	☐	☐
FIRST DISCARD		
Lavinthal	☐	☐
Odd/Even	☐	☐
_____	☐	☐
OTHER CARDING		
Smith Echo	☐	☐
Trump Suit Pref.	☐	
Foster Echo	☐	☐

SPECIAL CARDING ☐ PLEASE ASK

GENERAL APPROACH

Kaplan-Sheinwold
TWO OVER ONE: Game Forcing ☐ Game Forcing Except When Suit Rebid ☐
VERY LIGHT: Openings ☐ 3rd Hand ☐ Overcalls ☒ Preempts ☒
FORCING OPENING: 1♣ ☐ 2♣ ☒ Natural 2 Bids ☐ Other ☐_____

NOTRUMP OPENING BIDS

	2NT___20___to___21___
1NT	Puppet Stayman ☒
11½ to 14 3♣ _weak_____	**Transfer Responses:**
____to____ 3♦ _weak_____	Jacoby ☒ Texas ☒
5-card Major common ☐never 3♥ _forcing_	3♠ _ConFit_____
System on over _____ 3♠ _forcing_	___4♠ = MSS_____
2♣ Stayman ☒ Puppet ☐ ___cue = Stayman_	3NT _Gambling: AKQxxxx_
2♦ Transfer to ♥ ☒ BPH 4♦,4♥ Transfer ☒	_or AKJxxxxx, nothing_
Forcing Stayman ☒ BUPH Smolen ☐	_better than Qxx outside_
2♥ Transfer to ♠ ☒ BPH Lebensohl ☒ SASS	**Conventional NT Openings**
2♠ _MSS only if 1♣/♦ open_ Neg. Double ☐ ___	ROS = P → Redouble; Transfer
2NT _invitational_ Other: _____	Escapes; Baldwinsville Escapes

MAJOR OPENING 11+			MINOR OPENING 11+				
Expected Min. Length	4	5	Expected Min. Length	4	3	2	Other
1st/2nd	☐	☒	1♣	☐	☒	☐	☐
3rd/4th	☐	☒	1♦	☐	☒	☐	☐

RESPONSES

MAJOR	MINOR
Double Raise: Force ☐ Inv. ☒ Weak ☐	Double Raise: Force ☐ Inv ☐ Weak ☒
After Overcall: Force ☐ Inv. ☐ Weak ☒	After Overcall: Force ☐ Inv. ☐ Weak ☒
Conv. Raise: 2NT ☒ 3NT ☒ Splinter ☒	Forcing Raise: J/S in other minor ☐
Other _NS3=S, NS4=V, splinter=void_	Single raise ☒ Other _____
1NT: Forcing ☒ Semi-forcing ☒ BPH	Frequently bypass 4+ ♦ ☒ always
2NT: Forcing ☒ Inv. ☐ ____to_____	1NT/1♣ _6_ to _9_ exact 3-3-3-4 shape
3NT: _12+, 4 pcs., undisclosed singleton_	2NT Forcing ☐ Inv. ☐ _10_ to _12_
Drury ☐: Reverse ☐ 2-Way ☐ Fit ☐	3NT _13_ to _15_
Other _SSGT/PERR, power tries, funny raises_	Other _____

DESCRIBE	RESPONSES/REBIDS
2♣ _—_ to _—_ HCP	Crazy steps: 2♦=0-2, 3♣=3-4, 3♦=
Strong ☒ Other ☐ WOTOG	5-6, 2♥=7-8, 2♠=9-10, 3♥=11-12,
2♦ Resp: Neg ☐ Waiting ☐	3♠=13-14, 2NT=15-16, 3NT=17-18
2♦ _11_ to _15_ HCP Modified Roman	2NT asks shortness; suit = run-out
Natural ☐ Conv. ☒ (Mini-Roman)	2NT Force ☒ New Suit NF ☒
2♥ _5_ to _10_ HCP Undisciplined	WoJust: 3♣=5 pcs.; 3♦/♥/♠=6 pcs., bad/
Natural ☒ Conv. ☐ in any seat	med./good hand; 3NT= 6 pcs.,solid suit;
2♠ _5_ to _10_ HCP Undisciplined	After resp.r's 3♦ rebid, 3 steps=hand quality
Natural ☒ Conv. ☐ in any seat	2NT Force ☒ New Suit NF ☒

OTHER CONV. CALLS: New Minor Forcing ☐ _____ 2-Way NMF ☐ _____
Weak Jump Shifts ☒ after minor opening only 4th Suit Forcing: 1 Round ☒ Game ☐
Brozel at 3-level vs. 1NT; Burger-Harrington vs. Big Club; WQ asks full, promises
nothing; Ripstra vs. Gambling; Reverse CBS (2♦ = both, 2NT = neither); Suit-specific
Unusual Over Unusual; Invisible Cue Bids vs. Michaels & other multi-suited overcalls;
Burger-Harrington Cue Bids; After minor opening & 4th seat bid at 1-level: P=15-17
w/o stopper, 1NT=15-17 w. stopper; GSF; Inverted minors in comp. on iff both bids
available; 2♦/♥ xfer on after any bid showing strong NT; 4th seat weak two = 11-14
HCP; limit = 4+ pcs.; systems on opp. direct dbl. of 1NT opening.

Index